THE

PARENT'S GUIDE TO

THE DEFIANT CHILD

Dear Reader,

We've written this book to help parents like you understand and manage defiant behavior, whether it's due to
"nature" or "nurture" or some combination of both causes.
In fact, parents may not realize that some defiant children
have a real diagnosable condition called Oppositional
Defiance Disorder, or ODD.

Along the way, you'll encounter the mantra for Dr.
Kathy's practice: "I love you too much to let you do . . . ."
It's a key way to protect kids from dangerous situations and
behaviors while letting them know you love them and are
acting in their best interests. Dr. Kathleen Nickerson is a
licensed clinical psychologist in private practice in Newport
Beach, California, and has created innovative ways of
helping people with emotional issues online via
FeelBetterNetwork.com.

We hope that this book gives you "everything" you
need to cope and to help your child in a loving, informed
way.

Jesse Jayne Rutherford
Kathleen Nickerson, PhD

WELCOME TO THE

EVERYTHING®
PARENT'S GUIDES

Everything® Parent's Guides are a part of the bestselling *Everything®* series and cover common parenting issues like childhood illnesses and tantrums, as well as medical conditions like asthma and juvenile diabetes. These family-friendly books are designed to be a one-stop guide for parents. If you want authoritative information on specific topics not fully covered in other books, *Everything®* Parent's Guides are your perfect solution.

 Alerts

Urgent warnings

 Facts

Important snippets of information

 **Essentials**

Quick handy tips

 **Questions**

Answers to common questions

When you're done reading, you can finally say you know **EVERYTHING®**!

PUBLISHER Karen Cooper

DIRECTOR OF ACQUISITIONS AND INNOVATION Paula Munier

MANAGING EDITOR, EVERYTHING® SERIES Lisa Laing

COPY CHIEF Casey Ebert

ACQUISITIONS EDITOR Brett Palana-Shanahan

DEVELOPMENT EDITOR Brett Palana-Shanahan

EDITORIAL ASSISTANT Hillary Thompson

EVERYTHING® SERIES COVER DESIGNER Erin Alexander

LAYOUT DESIGNERS Colleen Cunningham, Elisabeth Lariviere, Ashley Vierra, Denise Wallace

Visit the entire Everything® series at *www.everything.com*

THE
EVERYTHING

PARENT'S GUIDE TO

THE
DEFIANT
CHILD

Reassuring advice to help your
child manage explosive
emotions and gain self-control

Jesse Jayne Rutherford and
Kathleen Nickerson, PhD

Avon, Massachusetts

For the wonderful Miss S. —J.J.R.
For Daryl, who has been the kind of child every parent wishes
they could have, the kind of parent everyone aspires to be, and the
kind of husband who inspires me each and every day. —K.N.

Copyright © 2010 by F+W Media, Inc.
All rights reserved. This book, or parts thereof, may not be reproduced
in any form without permission from the publisher; exceptions
are made for brief excerpts used in published reviews.

An Everything® Series Book.
Everything® and everything.com® are registered trademarks of F+W Media, Inc.

Published by Adams Media, a division of F+W Media, Inc.
57 Littlefield Street, Avon, MA 02322 U.S.A.
www.adamsmedia.com

ISBN 10: 1-60550-369-X
ISBN 13: 978-1-60550-369-1

Printed in the United States of America.

10 9 8 7 6 5 4 3 2 1

Library of Congress Cataloging-in-Publication Data
is available from the publisher.

This book is available at quantity discounts for bulk purchases.
For information, please call 1-800-289-0963.

All the examples and dialogues used in this book are fictional, and
have been created by the author to illustrate disciplinary situations.

Acknowledgments

We are indebted to the following individuals and organizations for their support in our lives and for guiding our understanding of this subject before or during the writing of this book: Dr. Jill Murray; Jose "Pepe" Montenegro of Gang Outreach Educational Strategies and Tactics (GOEST); Lt. Gil Owens of the South Carolina Highway Patrol and Tracey Bobowski; Diana Dessery Hensley; Steven Cox of TakeLessons.com; Chris Dwight, Nova Reed, and our entire amazing team at FeelBetterNetwork.com; Bob Diforio of D4EO Literary Agency; Brett Palana-Shanahan of Adams Media; Hogan Hilling; and Kenneth Markman, CEO, Global Brand Strategies for their support. In addition, we would like to thank our spouses and families for their love, support, and practical help—we love you and would not be able to do our work without you!

de·fi·ant (de,də-fi'-ənt) adj.
The behavior or attitude of opposition or obstinacy; unwilling to yield.

Contents

Introduction

Today, parents often struggle on their own to cope with the myriad issues that were usually absorbed, managed, and healed by a larger family unit in the past. Kids left to fend for themselves, or who bounce from one adult's care to another, or whose extended families are scattered around the country, are more likely to encounter tough emotional issues, and have fewer adults ready to help them cope.

Defiant behavior is one of these issues, so if your child is aggressively or passively defying your attempts to help him develop into a healthy, caring adult with skills for academic, professional, and interpersonal success, chances are you're feeling burned out, frustrated, and alone, even if you have an actively involved partner. That's the hard part about living in the twenty-first century. But there's a silver lining—keep reading.

There is more to being an effective parent and solving this problem than trying harder, giving more, staying up later, and stretching your resources further. You need to understand what could be factoring into your child's behavior, learn proven tips and strategies, and then rethink your approach so that you can work smarter, not harder, within your limits and constraints. In the twenty-first century, there is a wealth of information to help you do this.

As you'll discover in this book, there are dozens, if not hundreds of factors that can lead to defiant behavior, from your child's age to an easily crossed frustration threshold to a traumatic experience, and many more. Some of these issues, such as hearing problems, are easily found and nearly as easily improved. Other problems, such as anxiety, are more of a puzzle, and may take more management on your part to resolve, but they *can* be addressed, improved, and sometimes completely treated. What's more, many treatment styles are available to fit each unique child's situation.

Finally, there's another amazing characteristic of life in the twenty-first century: a large population. With six billion people on the planet, commonalities abound. Researchers are having a field day running data through their computers, and you and your child benefit. How? Because now there is enough information for researchers to say for very specific problems: "These programs work. These programs don't. These medications work. These medications don't." Are there errors and gray areas? Yes, but not as many as there used to be. So, you may feel alone, but there are *thousands* of other parents just like you, with the same questions and worries, and with children who need a little extra support and guidance.

With each passing year, research is giving people a clearer picture of humanity and how to solve common human problems. Child psychology is an area of intense research that has been reviewed for the content you're about to read. Use the information in this book to rethink your child's life and your own parenting style, and apply the tips to make simple yet powerful changes with the goal of raising a happier, healthier child who is comfortable with himself and possesses the skills to meet life's challenges.

CHAPTER 1

What Is Defiance?

B ecause parenting styles and individual children's personalities vary widely, it's not always easy to tell if a child's oppositional behavior is just a short phase that's a normal part of development, a purposeful habit, or part of a condition that needs closer attention. Parents are often concerned about being too rigid and wonder what they should put up with and what they should let slide. Understanding the nature of defiance and its future implications will help you understand your child's situation and how to help in a loving way.

Defiance in Action

Like many social and psychological problems, defiant behavior appears to have become more prevalent in recent years. Whether that increase is a result of more frequent labeling or an actual increase in defiant behavior, no one is exactly sure, but psychologists do have more information on defiance and have found more effective ways of correcting it.

This prevalence has influenced the psychological and legal communities to create their own definitions of defiance. Let's take a look at how they understand defiance, and what defiance looks like in different environments.

Psychological Definition

Psychologists consider defiant behavior to be a *recurring* pattern of defiant or oppositional behavior directed toward parents, teachers, or other authority figures. It is categorized as an "externalizing" issue, meaning it is concerned with the child's behavior toward others. In other words, defiance is a problem because it affects the child's relationships with others, especially those in positions of authority. You see defiance when children interact with others, even when no words are exchanged. No wonder lay people often call defiance "acting out."

You'll probably be relieved to know that some defiant behavior is normal. All children learn to flex their independence muscles by testing limits and while they're at it, their parents' threadbare nerves. Defiance is oppositional behavior. However, psychologists have identified an externalizing disorder called Oppositional Defiance Disorder (ODD), which needs more formalized treatment.

 Alert

There are two types of externalizing disorders, Oppositional Defiance Disorder (ODD) and Conduct Disorder (CD). Symptoms of CD are aggressive behaviors that violate others' basic rights and significantly impair the basic functioning of an environment like home, school, or extracurricular activities. Symptoms of CD include destruction of property, harming animals, and serious violations of age-appropriate rules.

Defiant Behavior at Home

You'll probably see defiance most often in your own home. When defiant behavior becomes constant and unavoidable, the home can become unpleasant for everyone who lives there. In fact, parents may frequently look for ways to escape, and find they enjoy their defiant child's company less and less.

A typical scenario: You've had a long day at work and come home not to rest and relax, but to prepare dinner at light speed, then monitor homework, and finally force your kids into bed before you spend your last free hour doing laundry and paying bills before falling into bed yourself. You ask your daughter in a pleasant voice, "Lauren, please set the table."

But after a few minutes Lauren hasn't appeared. You poke your head around the door and see she's playing a video game with the sound turned down. She's not supposed to be playing video games before her homework is finished! You repeat, in a more urgent tone, "Please set the table." There's no response until you walk over and turn off the monitor, and instead of cooperation you get a screaming tantrum that ends with kicking and "I hate you!" despite your admonitions and threats to take TV away for a week. Lauren has TV privileges revoked more often than not. All in all, it would have been easier to set the table yourself.

 **Question**

Does your child have a hearing problem?
If your child doesn't seem to hear your requests, it might be helpful to have her hearing checked at the pediatrician's. If your child is having a hard time hearing, it could give the appearance of oppositional behavior and lead to the frustration and depression that often influence it.

Defiant Behavior in Public

If you've experienced oppositional behavior at the grocery store, park, or worst of all, when you were a guest at someone else's house, you probably wanted to crawl under a rock in embarrassment as other people turned to stare and cluck their tongues (or maybe it just felt as if they were).

Having learned to push your buttons quite well at home, Lauren might up the ante by seeing what it takes to get you riled up in public. At a birthday party for a friend one Saturday, she gets up from the table with a forkful of cake and drippy ice cream. You start with an "I" statement and follow it with a request in a low voice: "Lauren, I'm worried that ice cream will drip on the floor and make a sticky mess. Please sit down at the table." "No!" she shouts. (No hearing problems here). "I don't want to have to put you in time out at the party," you explain. "Please sit down." The cake falls on the floor and she doesn't even make eye contact with you. "We're going to have to leave the party," you threaten, as she dashes outside to play on the slide, fork in hand, leaving you no choice but to follow and retrieve her.

Defiant Behavior at School

From the time your child starts kindergarten, she'll be at school for most of her waking hours for the rest of her childhood, leaving school authorities to deal with defiant behavior, for better or for worse. Though your daughter was once part of the advanced track, she was kicked out in eighth grade because of low grades. The low grades aren't because she's stupid—she has a bright mind and can get As when she wants—she just refuses to do her schoolwork.

 Essential

A great book that covers passive defiance is *If My Kid's So Nice . . . Why's He Driving ME Crazy?* written by Dr. James Sutton and published by a small press called Friendly Oaks Publications. Though the book was written several years ago, it's a great tool for understanding kids who seem to be throwing away talent and potential.

Today, you're called out of an important meeting because your daughter has refused to go to class at all. According to the vice principal, she's sitting on the quad, doing nothing at all, thirty minutes after the bell. This laziness certainly wasn't learned in your home, where both parents work full-time jobs they qualified for with advanced degrees. When the vice principal gave her a detention, she replied with a string of curse words that have now earned her a one-day suspension.

The Natural Causes of Defiance

At the crux of many scientific debates is the age-old "nature versus nurture" question. Basically, everyone wants to know why people do what they do. Is it because they're "born that way" or because outside influences shape them?

The jury's still out on a decisive answer, but so far it looks like people's behaviors are determined by *both* natural and environmental (nurture-related) factors. That's certainly true for defiant behavior, though you may find your child is more influenced by one type of factor than another.

Children Whose Parents Use Drugs and Alcohol

Drugs and alcohol are two factors that can influence defiant behavior and a host of other problems. If your child was a victim of Fetal Alcohol Syndrome or was exposed to drugs in utero or in early childhood, he might have impaired brain functioning that can be a factor in his defiant behavior.

Drugs and alcohol impair brain functioning in two ways: directly and indirectly. The substances can act directly by altering the brain's natural chemistry, slowing down its ability to process information—not a good way for healthy thinking to develop. They act indirectly while a child is "under the influence," because he's losing precious time to absorb crucial information and strengthen neural pathways.

Kids Who Abuse Substances

The same two tragic results occur when kids ingest substances on their own. As kids enter high school, the likelihood that they or their friends have tried alcohol or drugs increases. According to a study in the Bureau of Justice Statistics, about two-thirds of high school seniors have used alcohol at least once in the past year, and nearly a third have used marijuana in the same time frame.

While public awareness of these drugs has increased, it's easy to shrug off erratic behavior as "just a phase." If you think some strange behavior could be influenced by substance abuse (including alcohol), take action immediately. Begin by talking to your child and increasing supervision, and don't hesitate to take your child to the hospital if you think a medical emergency is occurring.

Defiant behavior may be a factor in your child's drug use, or drug use may be a factor in defiant behavior. Either way, drugs pose a much more immediate threat to your child's well-being than defiant behavior in and of itself, so don't look the other way.

Oppositional Defiance Disorder

Kids can be born with a predisposition to ODD, so ODD can be a natural cause for defiant behavior. Briefly, ODD is a condition that interferes with a kid's ability to function, has been going on for quite some time, and can is characterized by a short temper, frequent defiance of authorities and rules, annoying behavior, and a spiteful or angry attitude. You'll find more detailed information on ODD in Chapter 4.

 Fact

ODD is much more common in boys than girls. According to the *Handbook of Childhood Behavioral Issues*, three times more boys than girls are diagnosed with ODD before puberty. After puberty, the gap closes, with rates being about equal thereafter.

Organic (Brain) Issues

Defiant behavior can also stem from impaired brain functioning. A head injury, learning disability, or emotional or cognitive delay—anything that interferes with normal thought processes—can lead to defiant behavior.

Many people are surprised to learn that trauma can lead to impaired brain functioning. Anxiety, post-traumatic stress disorder (PTSD), depression, and other conditions resulting from trauma or violence can throw an adult for a loop, so imagine what they can do to a kid's ability to function and develop. Many people underestimate the debilitating nature of impaired brain functioning and conditions like these, insisting that the child "snap out of it" and "stop licking his wounds." This old-school tough talk ignores the lasting impact that a few years of depression can have on a child's life. What your parents or grandparents may have described as dealing with tragedy and moving on may actually have been ignoring tragedy and burying it in years of silent heartache instead.

The Environmental Causes of Defiance

Once you take on the responsibility of parenting, there's no going back and rewriting your child's genetic code, or erasing the trauma or chemical exposures an adopted child may have experienced before coming to your home. In other words, you have much more control over eliminating the environmental causes of defiance in your child's life.

Lifestyle

Your lifestyle may be crazy, rushed, and pressured—working parents, financial stress, an unsafe neighborhood, extended family spread across the continent, past tragedy or trauma, parents too tired or depressed to give their kids the attention they need—all of these circumstances can lead to emotions like anxiety, depression, and frustration that trigger defiant behavior in kids. Sometimes, defiant kids may even tell you what's bothering them, or consistently become defiant in response to the same triggering situations. Slowing down the hectic lifestyle so you can pay closer attention to your child's emotions and the situations that trigger them is key to helping your child.

A hectic lifestyle, even for affluent families, can be isolating and lonely for each individual in the family. While it may seem to parents with more immediate financial pressures that their hands are tied, if you have time to look at this book, you have time to implement several effective strategies to help your child. You may also be able to take advantage of free or low-cost interventions and treatments when necessary.

How Lifestyle Relates to Defiant Behavior

As a parent, your duty is to raise your child so she becomes a fulfilled, healthy adult, not to keep your kid entertained, occupied, or busy. Sometimes, a hectic lifestyle leaves no room for deep, sustained thought; loose, unstructured play; or low-pressure interactions within the family. While enriching activities are beneficial in many ways, so is a lack of schedule. If you and your family need more time together, and your child's obstinate behavior disrupts extracurricular activities, considering dropping them for awhile. Don't frame it as a punishment (e.g., "If you can't behave in band, I'm not paying for it anymore."), but as a desire to spend more time relaxing as a family.

 Question

How much does the busy schedule cost your family?
You might be surprised to learn that your family's busy schedule costs you hundreds of dollars per month. Add up how much you spend on extra-curricular activities every year and divide the total by twelve. Don't forget to include extras like season tickets to theme parks, uniforms, registration fees, eating out, and transportation.

Chances are, if you're highly stressed and already up to your limit with a certain young person's behavior, spending more time together doesn't sound appealing. But if you approach the issue now, you will have more time in the long run because you won't be spending so much time disciplining your child.

Is This Normal?

All preschoolers throw fits sometimes. All preteens gripe and sulk over rules they don't like. All teenagers butt heads with their parents once in awhile. To some extent, defiance is a normal part of development, a sign that a child is testing the rules and learning the limits.

That being said, there are definitely some behaviors that need more urgent attention, either because they're a symptom that your child could have ODD or another condition, or because the defiance is interfering with your family's functioning. As you consider your child's behaviors, bear in mind that each of the behaviors described below take place over an extended time period.

Preschool Children

Normal defiant behavior in preschool-aged children includes throwing fits or tantrums. As children learn how small they are and how important they are to you, they look for ways to gain some control over their lives, and fits are one way they can dig in their heels and try to exert control over a situation.

 Essential

If you need a little comic relief from parenting a toddler or preschooler, Christie Mellor's *The Three-Martini Playdate* is a tongue-in-cheek guide for infusing retro values into family life. Much of the book is silly, but in all seriousness, Mellor (herself the parent of two "darling little angels") urges parents to be firm about their own rights in the family.

However, just because tantrums are a normal part of development doesn't mean that you should cave every time your child throws one, or that you should have to live with constant embarrassment from public tantrums. Looking the other way because tantrums are normal is akin to the parents of a bully throwing up their hands and saying, "Well, what can we do? Boys will be boys."

On the other hand, if you've tried taking away just about every privilege in the book with no result, you're probably in need of some alternative solutions. If it seems like every unexpected circumstance in your child's life leads to a no-holds-barred, sound-barrier-breaking tantrum, and it's been going on for several weeks or months, the behavior is not normal. That doesn't necessarily mean that your child has ODD, but it does mean you need to take immediate action for your child's well-being as well as your own.

School-Age Children

Whining, griping, sulking, and occasional rule-breaking are all normal behaviors in the school-age child. Hurting other people or animals, destroying property, or creating such an environment of hostility and negativity over a period of weeks or months that other family members dread the child's presence, is not. Neither is consistent defiance to comply with requests and rules.

Even if the defiance is seemingly passive, it's still defiance (remember the example of the little girl who had selective hearing). In other words, "sins of omission" and seeming forgetfulness (if you have ruled out learning disabilities or are pretty sure the forgetfulness is selective) are probably causing you extreme annoyance and lots of stress in your family. These behaviors over a period of weeks or months warrant intervention.

Teens

So if every teen is defiant, and the nature of adolescence is to pull away from the family unit and establish independence, isn't all defiant behavior normal in teens? No. Like school-age children, teens need help if they defy authority and disregard rules and social norms consistently (passively or actively), hurt others, harm animals, damage property, start fires, engage in dangerous activities, or cause others around them to cower in their presence.

A teen who defies one big rule is exhibiting normal behavior, but a pattern of defiance over time is not normal. Just because a teen is as big as you are—or bigger—doesn't mean his brain has finished developing. Not until adulthood does the human brain complete crucial developments, and teens whose parents stand by the wayside will ultimately suffer. On some level, teens know this, and are waiting for you to step in and assure their safety by establishing healthy limits. Alas, a healthy balance isn't static: it's the gentle push and pull, the creative solutions to conflicts, and the less-than-perfect compromises that are intrinsic to a healthy parent-teen relationship.

Parenting Styles and Your Role as an Authority

Parenting styles differ from one generation to the next, from one culture or geographic area to another, and even between you and your own siblings. What works for you may not even work for your partner. However, parenting styles can be grouped into four useful categories.

Parenting Styles

Permissive parenting allows the child to do whatever she pleases. For example, Marlene's seven-year-old daughter Zoe has several allergies, including nut allergies. Zoe asks Marlene if she can have some of Marlene's 100-calorie cereal snack mix, and Marlene says no because it's her own diet food. Zoe takes a bag, and Marlene protests that the snack could contain nuts. Zoe eats some when her mother isn't looking. Several minutes later, Zoe reappears with a half-empty bag, and hasn't had an allergic reaction, so Marlene decides it must be okay. Contrary to popular belief, permissive parenting is not being "nice" or loving at all. It is not kind to let your child run the show and ignore what you say.

In dictatorial parenting, the parent makes the rules and enforces them because she's the boss. "Why can't I have another cookie? Why do I have to clean my room? Why can't I spend the night at Daphne's?" are all answered with a stock "Because I said so," reply. Noncompliance results in automatic punishment, because "if you give a kid an inch, he'll take a foot."

 Question

Are permissive and dictatorial parenting styles ever appropriate? Dr. Laura Walter Nathason, author of *The Portable Pediatrician*, says that permissive parenting is effective for infants and dictatorial parenting is effective for crawlers and toddlers. Infants don't need discipline, and crawlers and toddlers need to learn not just the specific rules you're teaching but also that you're the boss.

Abusive parenting is *never* acceptable. Abuse is defined as a wide-ranging pattern of behaviors: neglect, emotional abuse (often called mental abuse), physical abuse, and sexual abuse. While most people recognize sexual exploitation and locking kids in closets as abuse, it's important to realize that belittling a child, yelling at a child, withholding food, and many forms of physical punishment are considered abusive, including whipping. If you or your partner is abusing a child, please get help for yourself and your child *immediately*. Abusing a child will *not* put an end to defiant behavior or the issues behind it—it has extremely harmful consequences on your child's cognitive and emotional development, and in fact will often cause bad behavior to worsen or intensify.

The assertive parenting style is the most effective way to parent any child over the age of three or four. Like many other interpersonal relationships in your life, the parent-child relationship needs time and attention, and an emphasis on communication and respect for the feelings and rights of everyone involved. Each rule has a reason, and enforcement of the rules may not be wildly fun, but is fair.

Authority and Your Role

Sometimes, parents are reluctant to be assertive with their children for fear that they'll be resented later. Maybe a father remembers his own father as a judge-jury-executioner type who ruled the family with an iron fist, and doesn't want to hurt his own children the way his father hurt him. Maybe a mother who is passionate about art doesn't want to squelch her children's creativity by putting up boundaries and saying no every time her son has a daring idea.

Although you may not be 100 percent comfortable with the role of authority and its impact on your identity or what it means in a larger philosophical sense, it's important to realize that as a parent, your role is inherently one of authority. Your child needs authority from you for protection, guidance, and security.

Why You Should Help Your Child Now

If you're thinking it would be easier to stick with the status quo, you're right—for now. But later, the chickens that are today's unchecked defiant behavior will come home to roost in your family's nest. You, your partner, your other children, and most of all, the defiant child in question will pay a stiff price if you don't take action.

Your Child's Future

If your child's defiant behavior continues unabated, it will make getting along with others and complying with authority difficult his whole life. Not to put too blunt a point on it, if you don't help your child now, his defiance will likely be transferred to society at large. He will not have learned the consequences of defiance nor will he be reluctant to defy the law and others' rights, so crime becomes a real possibility for your child's future. Unfortunately, the law doesn't have a communication-based assertive approach, so if your child breaks a law and is caught, he could end up in prison, and no focus on the positives will be able to change that.

 Alert

Kids often mimic the behavior they've learned at home, including abuse. If someone in your family is abusing your child, your child is likely to look for abusive relationships as a teen and adult. Your child could become the victim or perpetrator of teenage dating violence, spousal abuse, and abuse of his own children in the future.

You can probably imagine what this will mean for your child's opportunities for higher learning or professional success. A life of crime and disregard for others doesn't usually go hand-in-hand with college graduation or promotions in white-collar professions. Neither does it bode well for your child's future romantic and family relationships—just imagine how much stress it would put on your marriage right now if your spouse were also regularly breaking the law, unconcerned by the consequences.

Your Relationship with Your Child

If you fail to take action on your child's behalf, no matter how unpleasant she might be, she'll know it and resent it. Again, your role as a parent includes "protector," and your child is counting on you to fulfill it. Failure to stick with her through these rough times will leave her feeling abandoned, realizing a child's greatest fear.

If you value your child's future well-being, not to mention her relationship with you personally, you must not wait to understand and stop defiant behavior in an assertive, loving way. The first thing you must do to help her is to deepen your bond with her.

CHAPTER 2

Bonding, Security, and Love

There's a song about saying I love you that tells the listener that words aren't enough to show love. It's the same with parent-child relationships. If you didn't love your child, you wouldn't be reading this book, but that being said, don't assume your child knows it and that you don't need to say so or show it. There are some concrete steps you can take to strengthen your bond with your child and make her feel more secure.

How Children Bond

All human beings need to bond with their parents and other caregivers as children. It's part of how people are wired for survival, like needing to eat or instinctually recoiling at the thought of a dip in an ice-cold lake or a kick to the shins. In the old days, if people in a family group didn't bond, they wouldn't need to stick together during a famine or an attack by animals, and they'd lose members of their group pretty quickly. Though it's not as obvious or immediate, the same holds true today.

Bonding and Attachment

There's a theory in psychology called "bonding and attachment theory" that was originally developed by a man named John Bowlby. Bowlby grew up in an upper-class family in England about a hundred years ago, and was raised by his nanny as a young child, then sent to boarding school. He had little contact with his mother and even less with his father. This lack of opportunity for connection in his family was the basis for developing his theory.

In a nutshell, Bowlby argued that kids need a strong attachment, or bond, with their caregivers in order to develop normally. Switching up the caregivers from one month to the next, or failing to respond to a child's emotional needs when in a caregiving role, will not result in a strong attachment. Generally, the relationship needs to be consistent and long term, and the younger the child, the more immediate and crucial her attachment needs are. It is imperative to understand that the child establishes *a primary bond with one caregiver*, and that bonds with all other people are subordinate.

 Essential

> Maslow's Hierarchy of Needs is a theory for ranking universal human needs from the most essential for survival to the least essential. The most essential needs are physical, like food; the least essential is the need for personal growth. Not only does family security appear in the second tier, but young children depend completely on their caregivers for first-tier needs.

Attachment theory, though it was developed more than fifty years ago, is still largely upheld today. Just letting a child sleep in your house and making sure she has food and water is not enough—nurturing your relationship with your child is what creates a strong bond.

Securely and Insecurely Bonded Kids

Strong attachment in early childhood gives a child a feeling of security from which she can grow, and forms her idea of how relationships should work. The caregiver and the child are highly communicative, and the caregiver responds to the child's physical and emotional needs. A kid with a strong long-term attachment to a primary caregiver is able to form healthy relationships later in life, and may be able to pursue creativity, problem-solving, and other less essential needs that help her grow as a person and feel fulfilled.

In contrast, failure by a primary and consistent caregiver to respond to a child's bids for bonding can create anxiety in the child, interrupt normal social development, and can even influence psychopathic behavior. In fact, there's a disorder called Reactive Attachment Disorder (RAD). A kid with RAD may fail to engage in age-appropriate social situations, or, on the other hand, try to form inappropriate relationships with just about anyone who comes her way.

How Kids Initiate Bonding

You may be surprised to know that kids actually initiate bonds with their caregivers. They do this by what's called "bidding." A "bid" is any attempt at engagement, whether it's a hug, throwing a fit to get your attention, or even some annoying behaviors like leaning on you while you're trying to clean the bathroom. (Before you guilt-trip yourself for ignoring your child's bids, be aware that you don't have to drop what you're doing to focus on your daughter if she hangs on you like a wet cape while you're trying to scrub the toilet.) Securely bonded kids bid less than insecurely bonded kids; they don't need it as much.

The most effective way to bond with your child and to decrease the annoyance level of the bids is to respond to the ones you like. If your child hugs you, and you see that hug and raise it a kiss, you're responding to your child's bid and strengthening your bond. If your child tries to tell you about her day while you're still working, and you wait five minutes and then listen fully, you're responding to her bid *and* teaching her to respect your time. If, on the other hand, you tell her you're busy and put off listening to her until she's too tired to talk, you're failing to respond to her bid. If you do that very often, you'll soon leave her feeling disconnected, like a raft floating in the middle of an ocean. You don't have to respond to every single bid, but you do have to respond to most of them.

If your child's bids for bonding are inappropriate, ill-timed, or downright infuriating, don't visibly respond to her. Go ahead and seethe inside, but keep a cool exterior. Make a mental note of what your child is doing, wait five minutes and see if you can catch her being good, then come forward with the hug, affirmation, or interaction she was looking for. Keep in mind this advice is for bonding only.

Bonding During Good Times

Obviously, you can't leave all bonding duties up to your child, especially as kids get older and the pull of social life is stronger. So how do *you* initiate bonding with your child? It's not about having fun together per se—you don't need trips to Disney World or enrollment in special activities together. It's also not about checking off chunks of time spent together, because you can spend an hour with your child and still avoid bonding. It's about the *quality* of your interaction. Engage. Pay attention. Don't check out from your kids mentally on a regular basis.

Bonding on Crazy Weekdays

Cooking dinner is much easier (not to mention faster and safer) without a two-year-old on your hip or a five-year-old standing on a wobbly chair, trying to stir spaghetti sauce for you. You don't necessarily have to cook together; there's no single activity that can guarantee a bonding experience. That being said, there is a technique you can use for a quick check-in with your child if, for example, you only have two hours between the time everyone gets home and the time your kid needs to go to bed.

"Five-minute freeze" is a technique in which you spend five full minutes *exclusively* engaged with each child. For most families, that's five or ten minutes of putting off whatever else is pressing on you, like returning phone calls or cooking dinner. Before or after dinner, or when you wake up your child but before she is out of bed, you can formally or informally—but routinely—spend five minutes with each child. If your child is young, a cuddle on the couch, no TV on, no staring out into space, works well. With school-age kids, you can participate in snack time, sitting down to share your child's crackers and juice, indoors or outdoors. With an older child or teen, especially if you're playing Family Taxicab every afternoon, you can settle for having your teen sit up front next to you (or in the driver's seat, if he is already driving) and turning off the radio, cell phone, and other wireless appendages for the duration of the ride. This rule has to apply to you, too—no phone calls. One of you will be paying attention to the road, but it can still work as a five-minute freeze if that's all you've got.

Bonding with Leisure

Leisure? What's that? If you're scoffing silently to yourself, you're not alone. Like others around the world, Americans have seen a huge decline in leisure time over the last thirty or so years. However, Americans still enjoy a relatively nice quality of life with some freedom over how to spend their time, if not on a day-to-day basis, then certainly in the grand scheme of things. In other words, you choose whether to sign up for pee wee soccer or to leave Saturdays open to spontaneity; you choose whether to stay up late or get up early to work out; you choose whether to get a dog that needs nightly walking or a cat that doesn't.

Determine how to spend some upcoming free time with all or part of your immediate family. Find a low-stress activity you can all engage in, such as a trip to a local park, a picnic in the grassy area of your housing development, or a walk on the beach or other open area. Make sure it allows for face-to-face time with your kid. For example, a long bike ride could be great if:

- It's in an area that allows you to ride close to your child
- You can hear each other and talk when you want

- You can stop whenever you want to take a drink of water or get a snack
- You as the adult are not focused on achieving a distance, speed, or educational goal during the ride
- Your child is excited about the ride and wants to do it
- You are relaxed about the ride rather than stressed or worked up about finding trails, parking, making your child comfortable, staying safe, etc.

In a structured lifestyle like the modern American one, "free" activities like going on a bike ride often are eschewed for prepaid, scheduled activities, like joining a cycling club. Sometimes, people even consider open-ended activities to be "wasting time." If you think that's the case for you, penciling in time for leisure isn't exactly the solution to not having it, but it can help you get there over time.

Bonding During Tough Times

Marital problems, financial stress, unexpected responsibilities, medical problems—all of these issues can leave you ill-equipped to deal with daily life, let alone a defiant child. If you're a worrier or find yourself increasingly distracted by other stressors, set aside certain times to think about them, and reserve other chunks of time when worrying or obsessive thoughts are off-limits and you can freely engage with your child.

After Trauma

If your child has suffered trauma through loss of a loved one, abuse, or catastrophe, take the pressure off of everyone and keep bonding situations low-key. Let your child pick an activity she'd like to do, and just be by her side while she does it. If at first she picks TV or videogames, it's not ideal, but it's okay for a while as long as it's not extremely distressing. Just watch it with her and be fully engaged. You can make nonjudgmental observations like,

"Wow, it's really getting to the good part now, huh?" or "What do you think is going to happen?" Emphasize that you want to be with your child, and demonstrate that you love her and will always be there for her. Gradually transition into nonmedia bonding activities as your family recovers.

 Question

How do you use "worry time?"
Matthew McKay's workbook *Thoughts and Feelings* can help you become more aware of your train of thought, pinpoint underlying troubles, and alleviate anxiety, panic attacks, excessive anger, and obsessive worrying. In a nutshell, corralling worry into preset times of the day will keep it from taking over your thoughts so you can function better.

Long Term

As your family recovers from trauma, keep the pressure low and let your child pick the activity when bonding. If your child wants to stay inside and work on a 3-D dinosaur puzzle, sit closely, and resist the urge to pick up the glue and pieces yourself while gently narrating what your child is doing. You might say, "Oh, you're getting out your paintbrush now," or, "Looks like you're figuring out how to fit those ribs together." Don't pick up anything unless your child specifically asks you to, and don't take on the role of expert, turning the activity into Dad's Paleontology Basics 101.

By the way, parents of teenagers can use these techniques for getting teens to talk more about what's going on in their lives. If you don't have an agenda for "finding out what that kid is up to," and you just spend some downtime together without specifying that you want to talk about serious issues, your teen may very well open up about her life without you having to prod her. Sometimes important discussions need to happen as well, and you can still have an agenda for those—just remember that they're different from bonding activities.

When Your Child Resists

Your child might think some of your attempts at bonding are insincere or corny, especially if you're trying something new after reading a parenting book, or if you've been separated for a time. He might act as if he doesn't even notice you're making an attempt. Or, your child might be resentful of you or blame you if your bond is not as strong as it could be. There are a few things you can do to succeed at bonding, and they all require a sustained effort on your part.

Try Again

If your child seems not to notice you while you're bonding, or if he doesn't want to do anything with you, don't give up. Nothing says "I mean it" like persistence. It's possible your child may be quite aware of what you're doing, but is reserving his feelings while watching to see what you do. This is especially likely, and frankly pretty smart, if your child has been burned before and is concerned about getting hurt again.

 Alert

Adaptive behaviors, like guarding one's emotions in order to protect them, can be a double-edged sword. Fortunately, people learn from their mistakes and are usually wary of those who have hurt them in the past. Unfortunately, however, withdrawing emotionally from family members and caregivers has devastating long-term consequences for your child's interpersonal skills.

It's important *not* to have an agenda for bonding activities. As indicated above, don't push for goals such as making ten three-pointers before leaving the court, or learning the names of five local birds on a nature walk. What's more, your goal of "bond with child in five minutes today" should be shelved, because if you are looking for a specific outcome, you'll probably be pretty disappointed, especially at first. Take it slow, and think of your five-minute freezes as individual one-dollar bills in a savings account: it takes awhile for them to amount to anything. Show your kid that you are in it with him for the long haul, and aren't just in his life for a little while because he did something *really* bad this time.

Try Something Else

If your child resists your attempts at bonding for a long time—say, two months or more—then explore changing your tactics. Instead of five-minute freezes, reserve longer chunks of time on a weekend. Or, if your child is so attached to his iPod that unplugging it is like unplugging *him*, see if you can live with his gizmo if the trade-off is a more peaceful household. These considerations are fine *as long as* you really do bond over time.

If your child resists everything you can come up with, try clustering some of the attempted activities to find a pattern. Have any of the following types of activities been more successful than others at strengthening your bond with your child?

- Outdoor activities, like running, swimming, biking
- Indoor activities like puzzles, cards, cooking, cleaning
- Cuddling, hugging, lying together at night while your child falls asleep
- Activities in the early morning instead of later in the day
- Activities in which you're side by side instead of face to face
- Predictable versus unpredictable situations and environments
- Stimulating activities like watching car races versus soothing activities like playing with a pet

Finding a pattern can help you mine a more promising vein. If you're disappointed that your kid doesn't share the same hobbies you do, your feeling is valid, but you can look forward to having new, unexpected experiences.

Love Styles

You might recoil at some suggestions for bonding because they don't sound like fun or just aren't "you." But after trying a few ways to bond, you'll probably find a good fit for your child, and hopefully for yourself, too. You also need to understand different love styles, how people express and receive love, to find what works best for your child. Gary Chapman, author of *The Five Love Languages*, has been a trailblazer in identifying different love styles. The first style, quality time, has been covered pretty thoroughly above. Below are some other styles your child may respond well to.

Giving Gifts

This is perhaps one of the most misunderstood ways of expressing love. It's important to have a clear concept of how gifts can and cannot express love, because everything in modern culture costs money. For this reason, giving gifts to a kid who prefers another love style can give her the impression you're trying to "buy" her.

Gifts are most effective for people who really value them as an expression of love. If your daughter melts over presents, you can give her a present now and then, "just because." Sticking within your budget and being sure that presents aren't a substitute for your attention or love are important considerations for the parent of a kid who loves gifts. Also, focus on gifts that appropriate and thoughtful, perhaps even those that don't cost a dime, like flowers you pick, cookies you bake, or handwritten postcards from a business trip.

Loving Words

Loving words are also misunderstood, often being dismissed as glib, slick, or simplistic. But for some people, compliments, praise, and words of love do wonders for the spirit. As a parent, you can say "I love your sense of style and the way you dress," "Give me five! Atta boy!" or "Look at the A you got on the spelling quiz! I'm so proud of you!" If your kid warms up to this kind of talk, ramp up the praise and pile on the compliments whenever possible. You can even send e-mails or texts to an older kid who's always plugged in.

Saying "I love you" is an exception. As kids get older, especially boys, many of them start to shy aware from the sheer mushiness of this phrase. Don't stop saying it at least once a day, even to kids who don't respond to it, because even the kid who sneers when you say it is glad to hear it.

Touching

Some people feel most loved when they are held, stroked, kissed, hugged, and otherwise lovingly touched. Frequent pats, tousles of the hair, and squeezes on the arm throughout the day make these children's hearts swell.

The increased awareness of child abuse has raised the "ick factor" for touching kids in even the most appropriate and loving ways. People who have no intent on abusing a child may often resist doling out lots of hugs because they worry onlookers will consider their exuberant physical displays of affection abusive. This is especially true for adults who themselves prefer touch over any other love style—they might feel grotesque or under-valued. Everyone needs to be touched, and if your kids don't like it as much as you do, find a level that's comfortable for everyone.

Obviously, all touch must be age- and sexually appropriate. As your child grows, you may even wish to point out how important touch is to her, so when she becomes sexually active she can be aware of how she judges others' behavior.

Favors

Loving favors are simple acts done to ease the life of another person. You might feel like you do plenty to ease your child's life as it is, and you probably do. But favors out of the ordinary help some kids feel loved. You could do one of your child's chores, fix a broken toy, move a heavy piece of furniture that's in the way of the closet, or do an Internet search to find operating instructions for a gizmo your kid is having problems with.

Parents of kids who value favors should make sure a favor is sincere. Don't do a chore that has been the cause of defiance by your child. Don't serve favors with a side of insults, à la "I did this because you haven't got the gumption to do it yourself." Instead, receive the child's thanks, if it's offered, with a simple "You're welcome" and a smile.

Bonds with Other Adults

If you realize that your child's primary bond is with another adult, feeling like you're second fiddle can be very painful, especially if the primary attachment is with a daycare provider or other individual outside of your family. What should you do if your child is strongly attached to someone else?

Respecting Healthy Bonds

As long as a bond is safe, healthy, and appropriate, you should consider leaving it in place and even nurturing it. For example, if your child has been at an in-home daycare as long as he can remember, the daycare provider is likely a hugely important figure in his life. As long as you approve of the daycare provider, the morals and values taught in the daycare, and the environment of the daycare, respect your child's bond with the provider.

 **Question**

How should you handle your emotions?
If you are in emotional pain because your child is attached to a caregiver outside your family, you may need to consider therapy to grieve some of your lost attachment to your child. Just as children suffer from not attaching to a caregiver, you can suffer from not attaching in a caregiving capacity.

Your child may benefit by your showing how much you value this bond. A card on the daycare provider's birthday is certainly appropriate, as is a Christmas gift and perhaps an invitation to dinner at your home. Belittling the daycare provider behind her back will confuse your child, and severing their bond can be highly traumatic.

Weaning from Unsatisfactory Bonds

Your child may form a bond that you feel is unsatisfactory for valid reasons. If you have legitimate reasons other than jealousy for concern—say, the nanny is elderly and will probably not be able to care for your child within a few months, you have to move, or you know you'll be breaking up with a boyfriend your kids love—you may need to wean your child of the bond.

Start by planning a decisive action a few weeks or months ahead of time, and talking about it with your partner, if applicable. Then give your child ample warning that you'll be spending less time with so-and-so by June or whenever you've decided the transition will take place. Explain your reason in age-appropriate terms. You might say: "I really like Steve, and I like the way he has treated you. But I can't be friends with him the way he needs me to," or "Mrs. McEntire's body is getting very old and tired. She's having a hard time seeing and hearing, and thinks that pretty soon you'll be running much faster than her." Or: "Next month I'm going to get a new job and we'll have to move to where it is. We're going to have some new places to explore and new people in our lives, and we'll also have to say goodbye to some places and people we know now."

Allow the conversation to develop as a dialogue over the next few days so there's time for the idea to sink in, and your child can say goodbye and grieve his loss, which will be very real. Gradually reduce the amount of time your child spends with the other person by spacing out phone calls or visits, if possible. Keep making bonding gestures at home. Remind your child of the transition every now and then by calling things to his attention, such as packing boxes for a move or giving back jewelry a boyfriend gave you.

Finally, when it's time to say goodbye, don't be gruff. Uphold your child's emotions and comfort him as best you can. If it's appropriate, encourage your child to make a card. Afterward, lower the bar for your child a little while he grieves and deals with the difficult transition. Be sure to continue making bonding gestures.

Separation from Unsafe Bonds

If your child has bonded with someone who puts him in danger, you will have to step in for your child's well-being and stop the contact swiftly. It will not be pleasant or easy, and will probably result in an initial increase in defiant behavior, because abrupt severance of bonds can be traumatic. However, once the transition is complete, you may find that defiant behavior decreases as your child adapts to a safer, more stable environment.

When faced with a tough decision like this, ask yourself which you prefer: your child's anger, or your child in danger. It's much better in the long run for your child's well-being and your parent-child relationship if you care enough about his safety that you're willing to endure his protests. Talk about the change to explain your decision in age-appropriate terms and to acknowledge your child's pain, and consider therapy to help your child grieve his loss. You can say something such as, "I love you too much to let you be around people who are doing drugs (or not watching you and protecting you, or making you feel uncomfortable, etc). Because of that, we're not going to be able to visit him anymore." Again, don't be gruff—remember that you're taking action because you care about your child and are sensitive to his needs, including his emotional ones.

Finally, remember that parenting is a marathon, not a sprint, so hang in there during the rough transition, make bonding gestures, and keep your eyes on the long-term goals.

CHAPTER 3

Health Problems

Oppositional Defiance Disorder (ODD), covered in depth in Chapter 4, is not the only disorder linked to defiant behavior. It can stem from a number of underlying factors you may not have considered: medical and mental health issues can play a role in a child's behavior, and taking a close look at these possibilities can help you better understand your child and meet his needs. Some of these issues have simple solutions; others don't, but no matter what the issue, if your child has another problem he can't define for you, you'll be on a much better track once you have an honest understanding of what you're dealing with.

Medical Reasons for Defiance

There are many medical problems that can cause a child to be cranky, irritable, aggressive, and unpredictable, and to seek out dangerous situations or high-stimulation environments. Take a close look at some possible medical reasons for defiance and ask yourself if you think any of them might be affecting your child. If so, you may wish to call these issues to your pediatrician's attention. Some of the problems can be more easily alleviated than others.

Problems You Might Alleviate

Sleep disorders are known to cause crankiness in kids of all ages. If your child does not sleep deeply, it could be affecting her ability to function and to behave herself. If your child sleeps less than others her age, or if she wakes up frequently, talk to a therapist and a pediatrician. Also, be aware that a change in sleep patterns—beginning to sleep more or less than usual—is a symptom of depression and drug use. Finally, kids' sleep patterns change at puberty as they begin to have trouble getting up in the morning and feel inclined to stay up later.

If your child has Type 1 or Type 2 diabetes, low blood sugar can be causing crankiness, spaced-out looks, and grumpy outbursts. Type 1 diabetes has nothing to do with diet, exercise, and obesity; it's an autoimmune disease that develops for reasons still not completely understood. Type 2, on the other hand, is a metabolic disease that particularly affects obese and sedentary children. Type 1 diabetes is more common in children, but Type 2 is more common overall.

 Essential

The Everything® Parent's Guide to Children with Juvenile Diabetes provides comprehensive, detailed information on managing symptoms of diabetes in kids. It also explains in greater detail the difference between each type of diabetes and some of the symptoms your child may present with, like excessive urination or bed-wetting.

Allergies and sensitivities can cause irritability and unpredictability in kids. No one knows for sure exactly why—though there are some strong theories—but allergies are much more common today than they were a generation ago. So, your child may be allergic to wheat, for example, even if no one else in your family is. Allergies and sensitivities that have not yet been detected are especially problematic, because they can cause weird behavior in kids without the kids or the parents knowing why. Think about your child's behavior and take note if it always happens just after a meal or just after going into the garage where toxic cleaning supplies and highly perfumed detergents are kept.

Abnormal hormone levels can cause aggressive behavior in kids. This is something that a pediatric specialist will need to test thoroughly before a diagnosis can be made. Before you fill any prescriptions, talk at length with the specialist, research the prescription and side effects, and then ask any other questions you may have.

Problems You Can't Alleviate

Unfortunately, there are some medical reasons for defiance that you can do little or nothing to fix. But, if you suspect one of these problems, take hope—you can help your child and even alleviate some of the *symptoms* through time and practice.

When the brain and nervous system don't function correctly, behavior is affected. Abnormal development of the brain and nervous system can result from genetic factors or reasons only a neurosurgeon can detect. However, head injuries and fetal exposure to drugs, alcohol, and tobacco—events that you or another caregiver might be aware of—can also impair brain development and cause aggressive or dangerous behavior. (Fetal exposure to drugs, alcohol, and tobacco is akin to a fetal brain injury.) Some people whose brain or nervous system development has been impaired have difficulty controlling their impulses. They may also require more sensory stimulation for their brains to function normally, leading them to seek out dangerous, exciting, or highly stimulating activities in order to feel good. Some of those activities could include run-ins with authority, fights, drug use, unprotected sex, and so on—all behaviors that can be called defiant.

Children are generally healthier than adults and can recover quickly from a cold, for example. That doesn't mean, however, that a child can "bounce back" when her brain hasn't developed normally. As a general rule, the key to helping a damaged nervous system function better is to move quickly so that there are no further impairments. You may not be able to change the past, but you can still change the future. If you suspect your child has impaired brain functioning, *act now* and consult a pediatric specialist.

Mental and Emotional Reasons

There are a number of mental and emotional factors that can lead to defiant behavior. Mental and emotional conditions fall in a field called mental health, or behavioral health, which is more of a "gray area" than medical health—there's no blood test for, say, obsessive-compulsive disorder—but there *are* concrete criteria for identifying these disorders. It is more difficult to determine whether the disorder is causing defiant behavior or is a result of the behavior.

Depression

Depression is a real and debilitating health problem. Affecting almost 10 percent of American adults each year, including about 8 percent of adolescents and about 2 percent of school-age children, depression is much more common than you might think. It is also more common in girls and women than in boys and men. While you can readily see that a depressed adult is feeling sad and blue, a depressed child often comes off as grumpy or irritable. What's more obvious is the child's loss of pleasure in previously enjoyed activities and his feeling of "I don't care." While depression carries a stigma that causes people to resist seeking help, it responds extremely well to treatment. There are a number of different treatment options that are effective, including medication and cognitive-behavioral therapy.

Sometimes it's hard to untangle whether a person is depressed because of the difficult obstacles he faces in life, or if his difficulties have stemmed from his depression. Unless there's an obvious event you can pinpoint, like a traumatic event or tragic loss, it's probably some of both. Depression becomes a kind of two-way street that is hard to separate from other factors. Trouble at home and school can cause depression, which will keep you from being able to move forward, and then you'll suffer and become more depressed because your ability to live a full, satisfying life is impaired, and so on. Think about this cycle long enough, and you'll see why depressed individuals are at a greater risk for suicide.

Anxiety Disorders

Anxiety is a common category of disorders that affect millions of people. Separation anxiety disorder, substance-induced anxiety disorder, obsessive-compulsive disorder, post-traumatic stress disorder (covered in Chapter 18), generalized anxiety disorder, and a host of phobias are all categorized as anxiety disorders.

People with anxiety can present with panic attacks, short periods of sudden, intense anxiety and feelings of fear or doom, which have symptoms of shortness of breath, chest pains, and heart palpitations. Obviously, it's not unusual for people to check themselves into an emergency room for some of these harmless symptoms. People with anxiety often are afraid they're going crazy and sometimes hesitate to seek treatment for fear it will be confirmed.

 Essential

Because anxiety encompasses such a wide range of disorders, with phobias being the largest sub-category among them, it's impossible to cover them in great depth here. You may wish to look at Wikipedia or FeelBetterNetwork.com for more comprehensive descriptions of anxiety disorders. A therapist treating anxiety may likely use a workbook, like the classic *Anxiety and Phobia Workbook* by Edmund Bourne, PhD.

People with anxiety often have "triggers," events that precipitate their anxiety. They can become excessively worried by watching the news, or they may be extremely fearful of animals, public places, flying, leaving their homes, and so on. The key to understanding anxiety is to realize that the anxious person really believes that extreme, terrible consequences will result from the object of his fear.

For this reason, anxiety is thoroughly unpleasant—terrifying, actually—for the person experiencing it. As with depression, you can't just tell someone who has anxiety to "snap out of it." He won't. You could actually make his condition worse if you give him the impression he should be able to control it alone and without treatment. If you think your child is suffering from anxiety, don't be ashamed or worry that you are somehow at fault. Instead, help him build skills for coping and alleviating anxiety by taking him to a therapist or psychologist for formal, proven-effective treatment.

Cognitive Reasons

There are also some cognitive reasons for defiant behavior. Some of these may be intertwined with medical reasons and even mental and emotional reasons. It's important to be honest with yourself and your partner about the full picture of your child's life, including cognitive delays or slow skill development and their impact on behavior.

Low IQ and Cognitive Delays

During the past twenty years or so, IQ has been dismissed in many circles as an inadequate measure of intelligence. "What is intelligence?" "How do we measure it?" and "What does a high score even mean?" are valid questions that force society to rethink how it labels and values others and how schools are structured.

These questions notwithstanding, for better or for worse, children who score low on IQ tests *tend* to do poorly in school compared to children who score high on IQ tests. It does *not* mean these children are stupid. It *does* mean that their grades are poorer. It *can* mean that they *feel* stupid because they relate poor grades to stupidity, or because people tell them or imply that they're stupid. In and of itself, feeling stupid and undervalued in a place she spends most of her waking hours being judged and graded is enough to make a child frustrated and grumpy.

If your child has a cognitive delay or mental handicap, this argument is even more powerful. What happens to a kid who spends a lot of time in separate classrooms or getting different components in her education, particularly if the classes are called "remedial," "special," or another new, more euphemistic term? You hope that the classes serve to close the learning gap and give her the skills she needs to ensure her future success. Be that as it may, her education is still obviously different, and being a kid, she may not be totally comfortable with being different, since different isn't cool until she's in her late teens and practically done growing up.

 Fact

Children who are deaf from birth or a young age cannot get full language input from reading lips or reading written English. In order to live a full life—with a stimulating education, enjoyment of the arts, and a thriving social life—deaf children need immersion in American Sign Language (ASL). Usually, this is at a school for the deaf.

Children with cognitive delays, especially those with language difficulties, may find it harder to express their feelings. It's hard enough for an adult to articulate existential angst, so imagine how hard it must be for a young child with a cognitive or language impairment. Frustration, anxiety, depression, or pent-up anger doesn't have much chance of being expressed in a healthy, healing way unless the child is given the tools to do so. A therapist can help.

Poor Social Skills

Some children with defiant behavior patterns lack social skills to help them succeed in school and extra-curricular activities. There are some kids who are born with the kind of charisma that draws people to them, and there are some who aren't. That doesn't mean that they're doomed to be outcasts, though, because social skills can be taught. Teaching kids appropriate social behavior and manners will help smooth the rough edges at home and in school, and once your child gets a taste of the payoff—a nice social life— she'll probably stick with it. A good axiom to keep in mind is: "In order to have friends, you have to be a friend." Ask your child if she would like to have more friends, and if you sense that she does, tell her that you can teach her some ways to make friends.

Here are some skills to work on with your child to build friendships and social alliances when she's ready:

- Asking before taking things from other people. To teach this, model the appropriate behavior and explain it to your child as you do so.
- Playing games for fun and spirit, not winning and losing. To teach this, play a board game as a family and focus on fun and interaction, not winning and losing.
- Making others feel welcome and valued. To teach this, invite another family for dinner. Explain to your child ahead of time how you, the adult, will treat your guests so they're comfortable—taking coats, offering food and drink, sharing the best seat on the couch—and ask if your child has ideas about how to help the younger guests feel comfortable. Carry out the visit with a lot of wink-winking between you and your child as you each perform the tasks you outlined ahead of time, and recap the evening later to talk about what went well and how the guests reacted.
- Being flexible in a group. To teach this, model the behavior by pointing it out to your child when you do so. Explain the difference between being flexible (going to a restaurant you don't like because you were outvoted) and putting yourself in danger (eating peanut butter sandwiches when you're allergic to peanut butter).

- Helping others in need. To teach this, model the behavior and explain it to your child. There is no need to work in a soup kitchen if you don't have time, but simple acts, like picking up newspapers piling up at the neighbors' house when they're out of town, take little effort.

You'll need to do a lot of narration with your child as you teach these skills to explain the reasons behind your behavior: "I really wanted to go to out for pizza after the game, but everybody else wanted hamburgers. So I said, okay, you know what? Hamburgers are fine this time—I can eat pizza some other time. It worked out well because I got to hang out with my friends, and while I was there, they invited me to go to another game next week. If I hadn't gone out for hamburgers, I would have missed out on that invitation."

Frustration
Sometimes kids act defiantly because they're easily frustrated and have a hard time explaining their feelings. One of the most helpful tools you can give your child is the word "frustrated." Sometimes the word "frustrated" doesn't come up in the basic naming of feelings like sad, mad, happy, tired, surprised, and hungry. Frustration is more complex, but kids definitely feel it.

If you see your child building up to a full-scale meltdown because she really wants to write her name but hasn't built the necessary skills to succeed (holding a pencil correctly, practicing the letters first), you can gently say, "It looks like you're feeling *frustrated* because you want to write your name but it's not working out like you wanted." If your child says yes or nods, you're on the right path. Naming the feeling is very important. Take it slow, empathize with the feeling—"Yes, that does sound frustrating"—and ask her if she would like to take a break or have you teach her the simple parts of writing her name that she needs to practice. Empathy and communication skills are covered in more depth in Chapter 8.

Where to Get an Exam or Screening

If you do suspect your child has a medical or mental health problem that could be causing defiant behavior, it's best to find a qualified professional to conduct testing. You'll have a number of different options.

How to Choose a Professional

If you suspect your child has had brain trauma, has an allergy or sensitivity, sleep disorder, abnormal hormone levels, cognitive delay, or diabetes, consult a pediatrician for testing or referrals to a specialist. You may also wish to consult a pediatrician if you suspect your child is using drugs and would like a blood or urine test. If you suspect your child has a language impairment, ask for a referral to a speech therapist or speech pathologist (your child's school district may employ a speech pathologist).

If, however, you suspect your child could be suffering from depression, or any type of anxiety, consult a mental health professional. The choices are: a marriage and family therapist (MFT), a licensed clinical psychologist, or a psychiatrist. Marriage and family therapists have the least training, and psychiatrists have the most extensive training and are the only ones who can prescribe medications. Look for a mental health professional in the yellow pages, by using an online search engine, or by visiting FeelBetterNetwork.com or PsychologyToday.com. Check to see that the professional's credentials are current and their license number is displayed on their website or in their literature. Your child's school counselor can perform a behavioral assessment, and some graduate schools, clinics, and county mental health agencies can do low-cost assessments. Whomever you choose, *it is extremely important that the clinician has extensive experience, if not a specialty, working with children.*

Online Exams

There is a plethora of online exams to assist you in assessing behavioral and mental health problems. While these are helpful, and some are scientifically sound, it's best to consider them a starting point rather than a final diagnosis. You can take the online quizzes and show the results to a professional for follow-up, though, as you'll see in the section below, you may wish to hold off initially.

Some online assessments are free, while others, especially those that are empirically validated (meaning they have been scientifically proven to be effective) cost money. In fact, you may find some empirically validated tests to be quite expensive, largely because they are copyrighted documents that took years of time, research, and effort to perfect, so most institutions must charge for them. In addition, tests like these often require a mental health professional to complete complex scoring and interpret the results. For these reasons, it's best to hold off on taking anything but a simple, free online test until a professional instructs you to.

What to Expect at an Exam or Screening

If you decide to have your child tested for a health problem, you'll need to know what to expect, how to make the testing work for you, and what will be expected of you as the parent.

How to Make Screening Work for You

You may have a pretty good idea of what's going on with your child by now—perhaps you've seen all the warning signs of drug use, or know that your child is depressed and why. Your child's school may have given you some potential diagnoses, too. And you may even have taken some online quizzes that turned up a diagnosis you've been suspecting for quite some time.

However, when you seek out a mental health professional, you should talk about the *behaviors* that concern you, not the diagnoses. During your initial phone call, say things like, "My child explodes over the littlest things," "My daughter is always grumpy and lately has started hitting people at home and at school," or "My son just won't do anything I ask without an all-out struggle and it's wearing me down," *as opposed to*, "I think my kid has ODD," "I'm worried that she could have ADHD," or "His teacher says he probably has conduct disorder and maybe depression."

This is to avoid biasing the professional. Lay out the facts—the behaviors and how they're affecting you, your family, and your child's environments—and let the professional consider them and recommend the appropriate tests. Ask questions about which tests will be done, and what they screen for.

Interviews

The mental health professional will need to interview you, your partner or another caregiver (like a divorced spouse) if available, and your child. Be patient here—it can take a couple of weeks to coordinate these appointments, get everyone into the office, and give the professional ample time in one-hour chunks to conduct in-depth interviews with each party and get a clear picture of what's going on.

 Question

How should divorced parents go about interviews?
By all means, if you can work together without creating more conflict, invite your ex-spouse to the interviews for the good of the child. If not, you can brief the ex-spouse on what's going on with a weekly phone call. If that won't work, tell the therapist you'll proceed on your own.

You will probably have interviews both with and without your child. If you are stuck in a toxic cycle of name-calling, blaming, and conflict with your child or spouse, try to use effective communication skills (see Chapter 8) in order to make the visit more efficient. Focus on behaviors ("He slams doors in my face") as opposed to vague explanations ("She's irresponsible"). Likewise, if you are working in tandem with another caregiver, focus on the specifics of what's not working ("I don't think my wife follows through on her threats of punishment") rather than blaming or vague explanations ("He wouldn't know. He never pays attention!"). Blaming and vague explanations open the door for more conflict and won't make good use of your time during the visit.

Tests

Your mental health professional will probably recommend a battery of empirically validated tests. These will likely include a general personality test, a test for depression, a test for anxiety, a test for academic achievement, and a specialty test or two, as for ADHD. As stated above, such tests are usually expensive and take time and savvy to score and interpret, and this is one reason why your appointments won't be free unless you've gone a low-cost route.

 Essential

Mental health professionals are bound by patient confidentiality laws. The only time they can disclose your information is if the court subpoenas records, if they have reason to believe a child is being abused, or if someone is at risk for committing suicide or homicide. Therefore, you can be completely open and honest with the professional about your child's case.

Most tests take about ten to twenty minutes each, and the professional will read them to a younger child. They are usually true-false or multiple choice format. If you omit or cover up information when providing the necessary background, like the child's sex, age, and so on, it can negate the validity of the test. It's important to be completely honest with the professional in order for a correct diagnosis to be made.

Talking to Your Child about an Exam or Screening

Whether you're going in for a physical or mental health screening or exam, you'll need to prepare your child for the event by explaining what he can expect. Though you might be afraid of a struggle, a surprise visit can cause further conflict, confusion, and fear for your child.

Provide Details Beforehand

Once you know what kind of tests have been recommended, find a calm, quiet time to talk, and sit down with your child. Tell him that he'll need to go to the doctor or mental health professional or both for some tests, and that you agree with the doctor and professional that the tests are the right thing to do. Ask your child what he knows about getting a test at the doctor's or other professional's office, and go from there. You may need to explain what the specialist or mental health professional is in terms your child can understand: "An allergist is a special kind of doctor who tests our bodies to find out if we have any allergies, and studies why allergies develop and how to manage them so they don't make us sick," or "A psychologist is a person who asks questions and listens to us talk about our feelings, and helps us better understand our feelings and how we get along with other people."

If your child will need a blood test, or for any reason will need to have a needle inserted or other potentially painful procedure, don't cover it up or gloss over it. Your child needs to trust you and know that you would never trick him.

If your child will take a written assessment test at the psychologist's office, you might help the child prepare by saying, "These tests aren't like the ones you take at school. On these tests, there are no right or wrong answers, and you can take as long as you like. There's nothing to study, and you won't be graded on them. The psychologist wants to see your answers so she knows how *you* feel and think about some things in your life."

A similar approach can help prepare your child for an in-person interview: "I think you've been feeling angry and frustrated a lot lately, and there are people called psychologists who can help with that. I talked to a psychologist named Dr. ____ a lot about you, and I really like her and think she can help. She'd really like to talk with you in person on Wednesday. My opinion is one thing, but she says since *you're* the expert on you, you should get a chance to talk to her, too." Acknowledging your child as the expert on himself gives him a sense of control over the testing and assessments.

Build Trust During and After

On the day of the exam or screening, take on a supportive role. You're there to offer comfort and support, to take the child to and from the appointment, to hold your child's hand if he lets you, and to explain anything scary or potentially worrisome before it happens. Do not negate your child's feelings or try to change answers a child has given on an assessment test, or argue with your child during an in-person interview. Wait for your chance to speak in turn, or follow up with the therapist later by phone.

 Question

What if my child doesn't want to go to the appointment?
If your child expresses fear, discomfort, or any other negative feelings, practice empathy. Empathy sounds almost condescendingly simple, but it works like a dream. If your child says, "I'm scared," acknowledge the feeling by repeating it: "You're scared."

After the exam or screening, congratulate your child on being brave and trying something new. Ask him what it was like and what he saw, heard, and felt during the exam or screening. A hug and praise, and perhaps even a bonding activity that speaks directly to your child's love style preference (see Chapter 2), can cement your approval of your child's behavior and make any subsequent visits a little easier.

What to Do after a Diagnosis

If your child has one or more diagnoses, it may take some time for you, your child, and your family to come to grips with the reality of a medical or mental health disorder. The adjustment won't be easy, but a diagnosis isn't the end of the world. In fact, it can provide a clear path for treatment and management of symptoms, if not for a cure.

Attend to Your Feelings

It is okay to feel grief, confusion, sadness, or anger over your child's medical or mental health diagnosis. Give yourself time to process the information and allow yourself to reach out to a trusted family member or friend—ideally someone who is not the parent of one of your child's friends—to talk about your feelings. A long-distance phone call, a few hours with your partner, or a couple of hours off from work for personal time are warranted here. So is a session or two with a counselor. You'll have to explore the idea of "normalcy" and your wish for you and your child to be like everyone else. The truth is, no one is really normal—everybody has her own cross to bear. Diagnoses just make problems clear, concrete "things" with a label on them.

Some people really do find comfort in a diagnosis, though. After a few weeks, if you haven't started falling apart, this could be the case with you. If your child's behavior has had you on the edge of a cliff for months or years, and you finally have a concrete reason why, the diagnosis could be a huge relief. It's okay to feel this way, too. In short, it's okay to feel *any* way you feel, any *time* you feel it.

How to Talk to Your Child about a Diagnosis

Let the doctor or mental health professional be the authority here. If possible, have the results given to you and your child at the same time, and be brave but not gruff. Sit together, hold hands, and be supportive of your child, because this diagnosis and this moment are all about her. You have your own feelings, valid and important, but you can't fall apart in front of her or give her the impression that a diagnosis is something you can't cope with or that threatens your lives or relationship. She needs to know that you are stronger than her so she can lean on you.

Ask questions, and let your child do the same. Ask about the recommended treatment and what the next steps are. Take the position that knowledge is helpful—the more you know about the diagnosis, the better you can help your child.

How to Talk to Others about a Diagnosis

Other people, like siblings, your partner, your parents and in-laws, the school, other caregivers, and friends and neighbors may have been affected by your child's behavior and need to know about the diagnosis. Talking to siblings and working with schools is covered in greater depth in Chapters 16 and 17.

Base the amount of information you share with others on how much time the person in question spends with your child. If your child goes to day care, has siblings, has a blended family in another home, or spends a lot of time at Grandma and Grandpa's on the weekends, these people should know about the diagnosis and any treatment. Your partner or co-parent needs to have all of the information as well.

Other people don't need to hear the whole story. Parents and in-laws who live far away or who you have little contact with can get the abbreviated version, adjusted to your comfort level, with more details before they come to visit. If you're having friends in for dinner, you might want to tell them when your child is out of earshot, "Our daughter has a medical condition that sometimes makes her lose her temper. We've just learned about it and we're starting treatment. I just wanted you to be prepared in case she gets upset over little things while you're here." People at the grocery store who witness a tantrum, on the other hand, don't need explanations. There are always "tskers," and there's not much you can do about them.

CHAPTER 4

Oppositional Defiance Disorder (ODD)

Not every defiant child has symptoms that fit the diagnosis of oppositional defiance disorder (ODD). However, if your child displays defiant behavior, it's important that you review the descriptions, symptoms, and prognosis of this disorder and ascertain whether your child has ODD, which needs treatment in addition to carefully planned parenting strategies.

What Is ODD?

An increasingly common behavioral disorder in children, ODD affects between 1 and 6 percent of children today. Before puberty, it's more common in boys, but after puberty it affects boys and girls at about the same rate, though you'll see that there is some discussion about *how* it affects the genders and ages differently.

Clinical Definition of ODD

According to the official diagnostic manual of the American Psychiatric Association (APA), a diagnosis of ODD can be made when a child frequently exhibits a pattern of four or more of the following behaviors for six months or more:

- Loss of temper
- Arguments with adults

- Active defiance of rules and requests
- Blaming of others for misbehavior
- Anger, resentment
- Spitefulness, vindictiveness
- Being deliberately annoying toward others, as well as being easily annoyed by others

Oppositional defiance disorder develops gradually, over a period of a few months or even years. Frequency, duration, and severity of the behaviors are all key in making a diagnosis of ODD; however, a diagnosis of ODD cannot be made if the child's symptoms point to conduct disorder. A diagnosis of ODD *can* be made if your child has attention deficit disorder or attention-deficit/hyperactivity disorder.

ODD versus Defiance: What's the Difference?

There's more of a continuum between run-of-the-mill defiance and behavior that warrants a diagnosis and treatment, than there is a clear dividing line. Because describing behaviors is largely subjunctive, and because they can vary in severity from one day to the next, it's hard for even the researchers at the APA to measure them. Largely, deciding whether a behavior occurs "often" or is "extremely" annoying instead of "moderately annoying" is up to you.

And that's important, because you and the rest of your family are the ones suffering every day, along with your defiant child. A therapist treating a child with ODD (and supporting the parents) will rely primarily on your reports of your child's behavior. If your child's behavior has you at your wit's end, and you or others in the house live in fear of the child or avoid him, it's likely that the behaviors *are* severe and frequent, as the criteria stipulate. Also, if your child is frequently in trouble with law enforcement or school authorities, or if his behaviors result in diminished school performance, loss of friends, or deterioration of family relationships, it's likely those behaviors are severe and frequent.

Why Diagnose?

Kids with ODD can get worse without professional intervention. This does not mean that your child is crazy or needs to be removed from your care, but it does mean that undertaking new parenting strategies is even more crucial, and those new strategies won't work on their own—you will need to seek treatment and support from a professional, like a licensed professional psychologist, psychiatrist, or Marriage and Family Therapist (MFT). It also means that your family is probably experiencing severe disruptions and that the parents and other siblings could likely benefit from the support, structure, and perspective that therapy can offer.

 Alert

Kids who are violent or could become violent need immediate professional help. If you find yourself wondering if your child would intentionally harm someone, or you hear your child threaten to do so or see your child hurting animals, find a therapist immediately and tell her about this observation in your first conversation.

Some parents may dread the label that ODD or another disorder puts on their child, and could delay seeking a diagnosis because of their fear of what it might mean for their child's future. It's important to be aware of your fears and treat them as valid—you love your child and don't want him labeled with a behavioral disorder on top of everything else your family is dealing with right now. However, it's important to realize that your child's behaviors already are what they are, and a diagnosis doesn't cause a disorder. In fact, a diagnosis may even provide some relief for you by validating your feelings of stress—if your child has ODD, it makes sense that you would be at the end of your rope with him, and you shouldn't feel guilty or that you're a bad parent if you're on edge all the time.

Other Possible Disorders

In addition, it's imperative that you find out if your child has ODD or another disorder so that you can undertake appropriate treatments and better understand your child. There are other disorders that your child could have or develop that could look like ODD, and there's a lot of overlap among some of these disorders.

Conduct Disorder

Conduct disorder (CD), is another "externalizing" disorder that affects approximately 2 percent of girls and 9 percent of boys. Conduct disorder is considered more extreme than ODD, and what looks like ODD at first can develop into CD over time if it goes untreated. Your child *cannot* have ODD and CD at the same time—if your child meets the criteria for both disorders, she probably has CD. There are four sets of diagnostic criteria for CD in the *DSM-IV*:

- Aggression to people and animals (like bullying, cruelty, use of weapons, rape, or assault)
- Destruction of property (including destruction by setting fires)
- Deceitfulness or theft (like shoplifting, breaking and entering, forgery, or conning people)
- Serious violations of rules (like running away, truancy, staying out late against the rules before age thirteen)

At least three of these criteria must be met within the past year, and at least one of them must be met in the last six months for a diagnosis of CD. Conduct disorder can be mild, moderate, or severe, and can develop at any time in childhood.

Attention-Deficit/Hyperactivity Disorder

One of the most famous childhood disorders is attention-deficit/hyperactivity disorder (ADHD). Your child *can* have ADHD and ODD at the same time. In fact, it's quite common to find these two disorders together: about half of kids with ADHD also have ODD. Kids with ADHD are described as having trouble staying on task, paying attention, waiting in line, following through after being given instructions, sitting still, and ignoring distractions. Not surprisingly, ADHD can be a huge obstacle to classroom learning if it's not treated effectively.

 Question

What's the difference between ADHD and ADD?
Attention deficit disorder, or ADD, is not listed as a separate diagnosis in the *DSM-IV*. When kids present with criteria for ADHD but the hyperactivity behaviors, like trouble sitting still, are less significant, it can fall under a subtype of ADHD called "predominantly inattentive." Lay people often call this ADD.

Though parents hesitate at the idea of giving their children medications for mental health disorders, ADHD usually responds well to medication—much better than ODD does. If your child has ADHD and ODD, you may wish to talk seriously with a child psychiatrist about pharmacological treatment for ADHD to reduce the number of behavioral issues you're trying to address through parenting strategies.

Mood Disorders

ODD also commonly occurs in kids who have mood disorders, like bipolar disorder and depression. Bipolar disorder has also been more widely recognized by the public in recent years, though it has been effectively diagnosed for a long time. A few generations ago, it was generally called "manic depression," and is characterized by extreme mood swings in which the person fluctuates from extreme elation to despair, though some people with bipolar disorder have small highs and much more extreme lows. People with bipolar disorder can be impulsive and reckless during the "highs," spending beyond their limits and entertaining delusions of grandeur; during "lows" they may become melancholy and even catatonic or suicidal. Bipolar disorder can be hereditary, affecting several people in one family, but it can also present in a child whose family does not have any history of the disorder. It responds well to medication, but usually can't be "cured." It is tricky to diagnose and many bipolar kids are misdiagnosed with CD, so if you suspect one of those two disorders, it's very important you have a psychologist or psychiatrist who specializes in children take a close look.

 Essential

Co-occurring, often intertwined disorders are called "comorbidities" and are extremely common. Vicious cycles of comorbidities like depression, anxiety, and alcoholism are difficult to treat and impact almost every aspect of a patient's life, as well as family function.

Depression is another disorder that often goes hand-in-hand with ODD. As human beings, children are capable of the full adult spectrum of human emotion, meaning they experience profound sadness after a loss, or ennui from time to time. However, it also means they can become depressed, and are unlikely to "just snap out of it."

People have a tendency to think children are like rubber—whatever happens to them just bounces off and they are okay. That's a simplification of child development that dangerously underestimates how children are affected by their environment. The truth is that kids are more like sponges than rubber, absorbing everything that happens to them. They may appear unaffected by loss (whether it's a death or other loss, like loss of a friend after a move) because they don't remember events the way adults do, or don't have the verbal skills to articulate their memories, but they still have feelings.

Depression in kids can look more like irritability than constant sadness. It's also characterized by a loss of interest in activities that used to be pleasurable, by feeling "blah," and by changes in appetite or sleep patterns. Depression can affect a person's ability to think and make decisions.

Warning Signs of ODD

Because ODD can look different at different ages of childhood, and because determining the severity and constancy of symptoms is so subjective, it's important to take a closer look at warning signs and how they play out in day-to-day life at home and at school. Pay attention to reports from teachers, after-school caregivers, and other adults in your child's life, as they can tell you more about how much your child's behavior is interfering with his ability to function, and can help a psychologist get a better picture of the child's symptoms.

Warning Signs in Young Children

It's difficult to ascribe defiant behavior to children under age three because, well, they call it "terrible twos" for a reason. Between ages three and six, your life might feel like the situations described below:

Zöe is a bright five-year-old who, at age two, took the initiative to learn numbers and letters, amazing her mom with her desire to learn. She's extremely gifted intellectually. Somewhere along the line, though, she has become increasingly "difficult," which makes her mom worried because kindergarten is just a few months away and she wants her to start school off on the right foot. There is one situation in particular that her mother dreads because she knows it triggers an explosive outburst and all-out power struggle: getting ready for day camp in the morning.

The trigger in this situation is transition from one activity to another. It's also a useful time for Zöe to get her mom's undivided attention and see just how far she can push the limits. Can she make mom late for work? What will happen if she doesn't get ready to go on time—will she get to stay home?

It's a warm summer morning, and Zöe's mom Melanie has an important meeting at work after she drops Zöe off at day camp. "Zöe, remember that today's swim day at day camp! Don't forget to pack your bathing suit and towel," she reminds her cheerfully. Zöe loves swimming, but Melanie's cheerfulness is a thin veneer over a feeling of dread because this is how the daily power struggle begins. Zöe scowls, but other than that, she doesn't seem to have heard. She's eating breakfast in her pajamas at a snail's pace as Melanie packs them both lunch while eating her own breakfast with one hand. A few minutes later, Melanie says, "Zöe, finish your breakfast and get your bathing suit *right now*, or you're going to be in big trouble." Zöe then says she doesn't want to go to camp, and Melanie responds by saying she doesn't have a choice, and if she's not ready to go in seven minutes, she'll have no TV for a week. Zöe responds to this by yelling, "I hate you!" She then dumps her cereal on the floor and stalks off to her room, pausing to knock over a vase of dried flowers in the living room on the way.

Warning Signs in School-Aged Children

Connor is a fourth-grade student who has ADHD and has always had trouble in school. His parents have helped him through it and given him strategies to do better, and Connor has stopped taking Ritalin. However, Connor's teacher has called his parents into the school a half-dozen times this year to discuss his disruptive behaviors, which are more than just the typical ADHD behaviors like trouble sitting still or careless inattention to tasks.

Today, his teacher tells Connor's parents that Connor has become aggressive, kicking a playground monitor who told him his turn on the monkey bars was over. He has also picked up some new swear words that he's used toward the teacher or other kids who protest his disruptive behaviors, and deliberately let the classroom mouse out of its cage during quiet reading time.

 Fact

Kids with ODD can have difficulty in their social lives. Other children who live in fear of a kid with ODD are unlikely to be friends with him, or to interact with him unless they are coerced or forced by an authority to include him.

Other kids are disdainful or fearful of him, and the teacher sounds and looks fed up. Connor's parents don't know what to say—he's started being aggressive at home, too. None of this was in the ADHD materials the child psychologist gave them two years ago when she first diagnosed him.

Warning Signs in Teens

Max has lived with his dad and his dad's girlfriend for the past seven years. Like his dad, he has always been considered terse and grumpy, and his dad's girlfriend is usually sort of afraid of him, though both adults try to include him in their meals and entertainment. Now that he's sixteen, he has a driver's license and resists being at their home at all. It's getting harder and harder to account for his whereabouts, and the adults worry he has warning signs of every teenage problem in the book: delinquency, bad grades, alcohol and drug use, sexual activity, and a general "attitude problem." Detention and even suspension are becoming a habit, with Max regularly mouthing off to teachers at school.

Whatever attempts at normalcy and structure they've tried to give him, it all falls apart the day Max is booked at the police station for throwing a rock at a police car. There's no denying that he's crossed a line from normal teenage defiance into crime, and what's worse is that Max shows no remorse, nonchalantly excusing his behavior by reasoning that the cop shouldn't have been staring at him.

Treatment for ODD

While ODD can't be cured per se, it can be effectively controlled to the point that the child's behavior is well within the norm for his age group. In fact, you may be relieved to know that treatment has been proven effective in a number of programs. Typically, treatment can be divided into pharmacological treatment (medications), and strategies and changes in the child's environment.

Pharmacological Treatment

Medication for behavioral problems can *suppress* symptoms. It can't obliterate an illness by killing offending bacteria like the medications you give your child when she's sick. If you decide to try medication, take the time to explain this concept to your spouse and anyone else sharing childcare: it's important to avoid skipping a dosage because the problem behaviors aren't suppressed once the medication is out of the bloodstream.

There isn't a single medication that's prescribed across the board for ODD. A clinician who evaluates your child will probably write a prescription designed to suppress the most disruptive behaviors your child displays.

If your child has aggressive behaviors, drugs that suppress aggression, like olanzapine, quetiapine, and risperidone (marketed as Zyprexa, Seroquel, and Risperdal, respectively) may be effective. Lithium carbonate and carbamazepine may also be effective. Also, if your child's aggression can be described as rage or lack of impulse control, anticonvulsants can be prescribed; these are carbamazepine and divalproex (Tegretol and Epival, respectively).

Depression is often treated with the antidepressants bupropion, imipramine, and nortriptyline (marketed as Wellbutrin, Tofranil, and Pamelor, respectively). Just because a prescription is written for a child does not mean that the FDA has approved its use for children. At present, many antidepressants are prescribed for children, but only fluoxetine (Prozac) has been approved for use in children. If a doctor or psychologist suggests a different antidepressant, ask why.

If your child also has ADHD, Ritalin may be prescribed. Ritalin is a household name because it is extremely effective at helping kids to focus on their tasks and get their work done, and so has been widely prescribed. Though it won't directly affect ODD, it can help with your child's overall behavioral problems. Be aware that a pediatrician can prescribe Ritalin or any other psychopharmaceutical based on a short doctor's visit. That's not ideal—a child with ODD needs her parent to have an extended talk with a mental/behavioral health professional, like a therapist, psychologist, or psychiatrist, so that all behaviors are carefully considered and medication, if any, is prescribed accurately.

 Alert

Prescriptions should be written by a child psychiatrist because there are very few drugs approved for use in children, and their side effects are significant. Therapists and psychologists cannot prescribe medications; pediatricians can, but don't have the experience or the time that psychiatrists have to accurately diagnosis and prescribe medications.

Some parents who are hesitant to trust the FDA or the pharmaceutical industry may be tempted to seek alternative medications, such as dietary supplements, vitamins, naturopathy, hormones, and so on. It is strongly recommended that you do not give your child *any* type of medication, including alternative medications, without a clinician's consent, and that you disclose *all* medications to the clinician on the first visit. It's important to understand that over-the-counter remedies often have not been tested for side effects, and though some alternative products include natural ingredients, they can include them in doses much higher than what's found in nature, and can have unintended, possibly dangerous side effects.

Therapy and Training

In all likelihood, in order to best help you and your child create a more peaceful and loving home, you will personally need to attend some therapy sessions. This doesn't mean that you are the source of the problem or that your parenting will be scrutinized and judged. It just means that of all people in the world, you are in the best position to help your child by changing her environment and helping her reduce ODD behaviors, so the therapist needs to talk to you.

At some point, the therapist may also wish to have sessions that include your child, or are private with your child. This can be especially effective at treating comorbidities like anxiety and depression, and teens may benefit from private sessions in which they can disclose and deal with related issues they may not want to share with their parents.

 Essential

One thing you can do immediately, is to verbally praise your child for the small stuff. Catch your child being good—even a little bit—and recognize it without sarcasm and backhanded compliments. While you're waiting for your therapist to give you more instruction, you can implement simple praise, and it will improve your relationship with your child.

In general, you can expect that a therapist will work with you to set up a program for dealing with defiant behavior that uses a system of rewards for positive behavior, trains your child to think through consequences of defiant behavior, and minimizes punishment. If you think that praising your child for the smallest progress would be condescending and unproductive, you're not alone. Most parents would like to see some cooperation, pronto, and even a little retribution. However, programs that focus on praise and reward have been *scientifically proven* to be much more effective at helping kids with ODD than traditional punishment.

While the programs a therapist gives you closely mirror what follows in the rest of this book, remember that if your child has been diagnosed with ODD, self-help won't be enough on its own. The support and expertise of a therapist will be crucial in ensuring your program works and any glitches are corrected.

Low-Cost Options

Ideally, you will be able to find professional help for your child. However, the reality is that many insurance companies don't pay enough to cover mental health treatment, if they cover it at all. If you do not have access to affordable health care coverage, you may be able to qualify for low-cost health care coverage through Medicaid or your state's insurance programs. To find out if you and your children qualify, visit *www.CoverageForAll.org.* If that doesn't work, and you have a therapist in mind, ask if she has a sliding fee scale or can work out some kind of other arrangement. Some therapists take pro bono cases.

You may also ask your child's school what type of counseling services they provide. If your child has a disability or mental health diagnosis and goes to a public school, she may qualify for special education benefits that could include the mental health treatment she needs. You won't know if you don't ask, so call the school and see what services are provided or where they can refer you for more help.

You can also call your county's mental health office and see if any low-cost services are provided. And finally, if you live in an area with a college or university where graduate or professional level psychology is taught, investigate to find out whether they offer clinics where graduate students render treatment under supervision by expert therapists. Sessions like this usually cost about ten to twenty dollars each.

Lifelong Implications of ODD

Behavioral disorders aren't cured, they're improved. That means that if your child is diagnosed with ODD, there will never be a day when he's fully "cured." Take hope in the fact that if you work consistently and diligently, you can very likely reach a point when his behavior no longer meets the criteria for diagnosis. However, if ODD continues untreated, it can develop into CD, which is more severe.

Prognosis and Recovery

If you and your family work in conjunction with a treatment professional who emphasizes strategy and changes in your child's environment, as well as some components that help your child with problem-solving and social skills training, you could be looking at a much more peaceful life in as little as a few months. Noticeable differences may occur in a week or two if you work on one small goal at a time. It's important not to try to solve all behavior problems at once, to keep your goals behavior-specific, and to start with what's most disruptive for your family.

 Alert

Treatments that *don't* work, and can even backfire, include scaring the child with a visit to a prison or detention facility to show him how terrible it is, physical punishment, and peer group interventions. If your child's therapist suggests any of these treatments for ODD or CD, it's probably time to find a new therapist.

Once your child's behavior has changed enough to make his life easier for him and everyone else around, you should follow your therapist's advice for when to phase out the new behavior programs. After a while, your child's new habits will start to "stick" and you can focus on enriching his life instead of playing catch-up.

Development into CD

If your child's behavior begins to worsen, or if your child has been previously diagnosed with ODD and you think a diagnosis of CD is more accurate, it's imperative to seek immediate help. In about 75 percent of cases where ODD goes untreated, it develops into CD. Like ODD, CD develops gradually, with less severe behaviors emerging first. It responds to many of the same kinds of treatment and medications that ODD responds to, but not as easily, and the toll on the family is worse because the negative and even violent behaviors can be so severe.

Children with CD are known to damage the homes they live in, have frequent run-ins with the law, and put their families in physical danger—as well as themselves. If your child *ever* makes a threat or allusion to suicide, please take it seriously and call 9-1-1 *immediately*. Studies have found that most people who commit suicide tell at least one person before they do it, and teens who contemplate suicide should not be ignored by reasoning that they're just "trying to get attention." If the only way a kid can get the kind of attention he's after is to talk about suicide, then it's best to assume he *is* considering it and is crying out for help.

ODD Demographics

There has been very little research on the effect ethnicity, culture, socioeconomic status, or urban/suburban/rural lifestyles have on ODD. Demographics on age and gender are known: ODD affects more boys than girls until puberty, and then affects the genders about equally.

ODD and Boys

Before puberty, ODD is more common in boys. Not surprisingly, so is ADHD, so if you have a young son who has ADHD, you'll need to look carefully at his behaviors and consider the strong possibility that he could also have ODD.

Though the rates are about equal after puberty, the types of defiant behaviors vary widely between boys and girls. Boys typically will display more confrontational and aggressive behavior as part of ODD. And, sadly, more boys are found to have CD, so if you have a boy, you'll need to work quickly to make sure his behavior does not develop into CD. When you enlist the help of a professional, share your concerns about ADHD and any worsening behaviors that could point to CD.

ODD and Girls

Parents of girls who have ODD may feel especially frustrated because ODD behaviors are not considered very feminine. Acting out, defying adults, losing her temper—these behaviors aren't considered "ladylike" or "sugar 'n' spice." Admonishing your daughter to "be nice" and behave "like a young lady" are probably not going to be effective at fixing her behavior, and could even cause her to question her identity as a girl. For example, if your daughter often swears at you, and you usually tell her that she's not speaking in a very ladylike way, after a while she might conclude that she must not be very ladylike. It will be better for her in the long run to focus on her specific behaviors, as your therapist will probably suggest, rather than on labels or societal expectations. It could also help if you are careful not to set a double standard for your daughter and any boys in the house; if boys are allowed to swear and she isn't, then she could become more angry and frustrated.

Though there is not enough data to make a strong case, aggressive, confrontational behavior in girls could be rising with the popularity of "girl tough." In other words, if it has become more socially acceptable for girls to be aggressive, you may begin to see defiance manifested in more confrontational and aggressive behaviors in girls than you did when you were a child.

CHAPTER 5

Praise and Reward

Perhaps the most effective strategy you have to influence your child's behavior for the better is to acknowledge and affirm appropriate, desirable behaviors through praise and reward. To the parent of a defiant child, this, like bonding activities, may at first sound counterproductive, even insincere. However, if your child's defiant behavior is getting the best of you, and what you've been trying isn't working, it's time to trust in proven expertise and try what works. And that begins with praise and reward.

How Kids and Teens Respond to Praise and Rewards

Behaviorism is a branch of psychology theorizing that positive reinforcement of behaviors increases the likelihood that they'll happen again. So, if you're learning to ride a bike and pushing the pedal makes it go forward, your action (pushing the pedal) works like a reward (you get what you wanted: to make the bike go). The same can happen with your child's behaviors.

Rewards and Your Child's Brain

A bike moving forward is its own reward. Now you, as the parent, have to *be* the moving bike, so to speak, by rewarding positive behaviors. The result? You get more of the behaviors you want. This isn't manipulation any more than punishment is a manipulation—it's just guiding your child to do more of what you want.

Positive reinforcement is *extremely* powerful, more so than negative reinforcement. If you're reading this book, you may feel that the last thing your child needs is anything but a stiff dose of consequences. However, this chapter comes before consequences because positive reinforcement is simply more effective.

Everyone Seeks Rewards

All people—adults, children, men and women, all over the world—seek reward. On some level, all people behave the way they do because they want rewards for the behavior. Why hold down a job? Because people like to be paid money so they can buy things, like food (a huge biological reward) and new cars (a convenience and status symbol that are also attractive rewards). Why obey the law? Presumably, most people aren't *just* avoiding the negative consequences of prison and fines, they're also enjoying the reward of living in a relatively peaceful community and being respected by their peers as law-abiding citizens.

And why care about a kid who doesn't seem to care about you? Because there are several rewards: living in a peaceful household, pride in the future prospect of having raised a self-sufficient and well-rounded adult, and a biological reward for being part of a family that functions to serve the biological needs of everyone in it. That's a warm-and-fuzzy breakdown of a cold look at biology and psychology.

Behaviorism Meets Personality

Behaviorism originally held that people behave as they do because they've been conditioned to do so. That oversimplified things a bit because to some extent, personality comes into play. People are not exactly blank slates—at some point during a conflict, a frustrated spouse or parent has probably told you, "You're just like your dad/uncle/mom/grandma!" You may have even said the same thing about your child.

A cake is good analogy for understanding how far you can modify your child's behavior. When your child is born, it's like taking a cake out of the oven—it's already vanilla, butter, chocolate, or coconut flavor. You can decorate it anyway you want, with any flavor, quantity, or color of frosting, and you can even slice it apart and add filling, but you can't change the flavor of the cake. You just want that cake to be the best cake it can be when you're done with it.

So, as you think about your expectations for your child's behavior, keep in mind that some things will be easier for him than others, and get ready to be patient for the tougher situations. Is there another person in the family who behaves similarly to your child (possibly you)? If so, what kinds of strategies have helped that person? By observing the whole picture, you will be more effective at getting what you want for your child and your family.

Social Learning Theory

Social learning theory is another psychological philosophy that can be helpful in getting more of what you want. This is the theory that people learn by observing others. While there are many learning styles, and an education specialist will probably give you lots more information on this topic, for the purposes of behavior modification, think of it as "People learn by example."

 Alert

Social learning theory is another reason you might have for rethinking the bonds your child is forming with other adults you don't know. What's your daughter picking up at day care? What does your son learn from being at the neighbors' house all afternoon? Look for adults whose values mirror yours, and you'll be more comfortable with your child being around them.

That means that your child mimics your behaviors, as well as those of others and the society at large. If you are stubborn and unapproachable, your child will probably pick that up. If the grown-ups in your family eat fast food and sit around in front of the TV every evening, they set an example that won't be negated by telling your kid to eat vegetables and exercise. The "do as I say, not as I do" strategy doesn't work, or at least doesn't have much sticking power.

How to Use Praise

Praise is a verbal reward that you give your child after she's done something you like and want to see repeated. If you do it right, and do it often, it means a lot and is effective as part of a behavior modification strategy.

Direct Praise

Direct praise is praise that you give your child, rather than praise that she overhears. Direct praise is important and is most effective when it is *behavior-specific*, rather than labeling the child or focusing on a vague characteristic. So, "Wow! I see that you picked up all your toys and even found a neat way to stack up the things that didn't fit in the toy box—thank you," is much more powerful than "Wow, you sure are nice boy." By focusing on specific behaviors, you're being very clear about what it is you like and want more of. You'll have to pay attention to your child and really observe what she's doing in order to catch these and build them up.

Timing and frequency of praise are also important. You have to catch your child in the act and give the praise as soon as the behavior is completed, or as soon as you know about it, and you must do it every time you see what you like. If you're worn out by trying to stop problem behaviors, it may be difficult to find the energy to focus on the positive; if so, you can start by setting a timer for thirty-minute increments to stop what you're doing and observe any positive behaviors.

Here are some samples of effective praise:

- "I know you were very excited to go to the soccer game, but you still waited for everybody to finish dinner. Thanks for being patient."
- "You got a B+ on your math quiz? Wow, that's great! Isn't that a whole grade higher than your last quiz?"
- "Thanks for sharing your toys with your baby brother today. I was very proud to see you cared about him and were thinking of what he might like."
- "I know you don't like doing your chores, so I feel really proud of the responsibility you showed by taking out the trash without being reminded."

Indirect Praise

Indirect praise—praise of your child to others when she can overhear you—is also effective, but not on its own. If you're already praising your child directly, then you can add some indirect praise when you call grandparents, talk to your friends, or run into an acquaintance at the grocery store. If your daughter has previously been the subject of lots of negative conversations over the last few months, indirect praise will be music to her ears.

 Alert

Publicly complaining about teenagers is a harmful but common practice many parents engage in. If you need to vent, do so to close friends you trust and not in a public place; otherwise, your negative comments could make their way full circle to your teen and start a new round of conflict between you.

Indirect praise, though it's delayed, still needs to be behavior-specific and sincere, like direct praise. When your daughter overhears you saying, "She's doing great! She just cleaned out her grandma's garage for her—it was so generous of her," or "We're so proud of her—she's starting high school in a month and has signed up for math, music, history, Spanish—all kinds of exciting stuff!" she'll swell with pride and know exactly which types of behaviors (favors for Grandma, effort in school) you and other adults approve of.

What Doesn't Work

If, however, you add little digs to praise, such as, "Don't let that get to your head," or sarcastic reminders of past failures, like "You did great eating your vegetables tonight. Not like *last* night . . ." you might as well scrap the praise completely. It needs to be sincere and 100 percent positive for it to be effective.

Praise is also ineffective when you use it to compare your child to other people and show her that her efforts aren't quite enough. Comments like, "You're getting better at soccer. Maybe *someday* you'll be as good as your cousin," are actually praise of the *other* person, not your child. Your child will feel like her efforts are never enough to please you, and will likely resent the other person you're comparing her to.

Your Reward System

Now it's time to choose some appropriate rewards and put them into play. When you choose rewards, make sure that, like bonding activities, they cater to your child's tastes and are not thinly disguised rewards for yourself.

Choosing Rewards Ahead of Time

Choose rewards now, before you need them. Rewards should be attractive to the child, specific, tangible, and measurable, and they should be small and inexpensive enough that you can hand them out every time a desired behavior occurs. Think of rewards as analogous to peanuts for an elephant: you give one small peanut at a time, leading the elephant through the zoo step by step. You don't give the elephant a whole bag of peanuts at once—he'd stop dead in his tracks. A peanut for every step keeps him going.

For rewards, you need some "peanuts" of your own: stickers; small, inexpensive toys that complement a larger set and that you can hand out individually (like Legos); "bucks" that your child can use to "buy" extra screen time, time alone with Mom or Dad, or lights-on minutes; or even small pieces of candy, which can be effective but have obvious drawbacks. Whatever the reward, your child should like it and be able to understand what it is, and count it as it accumulates. What *won't* work: a new bike (too much) or some stocks (not tangible, not fun).

Setting Up the Reward System

It's all about visuals here. You need an at-a-glance reward system. For small children, use a chart or calendar for stickers, and keep it on the fridge or in another conspicuous place. Your child can feel proud to see his stickers every time he walks by. Or, if you're using Legos, keep the bin of Legos out of reach, and keep your child's earned Legos in a bucket that reveals instantly how many it contains. If you decide to go with candy, show the bag to your child once when you announce your rewards system, and then keep it out of reach, taking the bag down only to remove one piece of candy at a time when it's earned.

 Essential

Don't take rewards back. Once your child has earned them, they're his. Unless you're using some kind of a point system where your child "cashes in" his points to get a bigger prize, what he earns is for keeps, no matter how terrible his subsequent behavior. Remember that the rewards are peanuts and your goals for better behavior are long-term, not short-term.

For older children, you can use points, "bucks," tickets, or tokens that accumulate and are cashed in for something your older child will probably value more than stickers, Legos, or candy. The older a child, the more you can use this goal-oriented approach. For example, you can put a chart on the fridge that lists some desired behaviors (like complying with a request the first time it's made, or going to bed on time) in columns, and the days of the week in rows. Every time the behavior occurs, the parent makes a checkmark in the appropriate square. Ten checkmarks equal a half-hour extra for staying out on a weekend, or a half-hour more screen time. You can also use a jar of tokens, paper money, or a roll of tickets, as long as the accumulated items are kept in a conspicuous place, like a shelf above the sink.

Once you have decided on the best reward system, explain it to your child. Don't mention bad or undesirable behaviors, or what will happen if the child doesn't comply, just say, "Look, here are some Legos. Every time you use the bathroom on your own, you get one Lego," or "This is a reward chart. For every day you complete your homework and turn it in at school, you'll get a point. Ten points equals a half-hour of extended curfew on a weekend." Focus on one or two desired behaviors—whatever's most pressing—and leave the rest alone for now.

Tapering Off

At first, you'll need to be extremely diligent about giving rewards every time the desired behavior occurs. For one thing, your child may be skeptical about your sincerity, and may be watching to see if you'll give up on this and let him continue to act out. For another thing, the best way to form the habits you want is to reinforce them regularly and, if not immediately, then as soon as you find out about them.

After the desired behavior becomes automatic, and you have celebrated it extensively and regularly by rewarding it every time, you can ease off. Gradually give the reward less frequently, and taper down to praise, finally reducing it to just a smile. If your child has accumulated a large amount of stickers or Legos, admire the accumulation and all the hard work it represents. Tell your child how proud you are of his hard work. You can even take a picture of him standing next to a full sticker chart or bucket of Legos, and tape the picture to the fridge or other conspicuous place. Once you feel your child is ready, you can move on to the next positive behavior. Kids like star charts once they get used to them, so you can sub out the old behaviors for new ones that need improvement when it's time.

How to Use Privileges

Privileges are not rights; they're special, enjoyable, or even exciting activities or accesses to material objects. Staying up late, spending the night at a friend's, or using the Internet are privileges. Privileges are not tangible, and so they are more effective as rewards for older children.

Granting Privileges

In contrast to rewards, which are a one-time occurrence, privileges can be ongoing. Privileges are most effective if they are time-limited or performance-based; for example, your daughter gets to stay up until 10:00 P.M. on weekends for each week that she turns in all her homework, or your son gets to play basketball as long as he maintains a B average.

The younger your child, the more you need to bring privileges from the abstract realm into the concrete realm by use of a visually based chart or points system. Keeping track of points shows that your granting of privileges is not arbitrary; a chart shows that privileges correspond to concrete logic that's fair and predictable. Older children can think ahead a little more, and so rewards can take more work—but not too much—to earn.

As your child grows older, you will probably be taken off guard by all kinds of requests for privileges you've not prepared for: "Can I buy a brand-new car if I get a job?" "Is it okay if I spend Thanksgiving at my boyfriend's house?" "Would you be mad if I put food coloring in the pool?" and so on. Don't let your child put you on the spot—you don't have to answer immediately. Tell your child you need time to think about it or to talk it over with your partner, and you'll get back to her in an hour or the next day. Then look at your reward system and see if your child has been complying with requests for desired behaviors. If performance has been so-so, you can offer to switch the new privilege for an old one; it it's been great, you can grant it; if it's not so hot, you can say no and point to the specifics as an explanation.

Removing Privileges

Don't take back a privilege that has been earned as a one-time reward. If good behavior has earned your daughter permission to stay out late that night, and then she behaves badly, don't take away the one night of extended curfew you've already granted.

What you can and should do, is remove the ongoing, time-based or performance-based privileges. If you've agreed that your daughter is expected to maintain a B average in order to play basketball, and her report card shows a C average, take away the privilege immediately and until the next report card comes in—even if it's the middle of the season and your daughter is starting point guard with state championships coming up next week.

Don't feel bad if you have to take away privileges. Once you state them explicitly, your child has total control over whether to earn them or not, and it is not your fault if she doesn't come through for herself. If you don't take away privileges, you're not giving your child the opportunity to learn how to plan ahead or to form the habits you've requested in the first place.

Rewards Versus Rights, Gifts, and Bribes

Rewards should not be confused with rights, gifts, or bribes. In order for your reward system to be effective, and for your relationship with your child to thrive, you'll need to understand the difference between each concept and how to respect your child's rights while using gifts appropriately and avoiding bribes completely.

Basic Rights

Obviously, your child has the right to eat, drink, live in safety, sleep at night, have clothes to wear, and so on. In addition, your child has the right to an education, so don't consider a regular school day as a privilege for the purposes of modifying behavior. Extra-curricular activities like band, however, are privileges.

 Alert

> If someone who cares for your child is withholding basic necessities like food in an attempt to modify your child's behavior, remove your child from that person's care immediately and call Child Protective Services or the police. Withholding basic necessities is child abuse.

In addition, your child has the right to some form of enrichment or hope in life. You don't need to sign up for expensive lessons or send him to a private school in Switzerland. Within your budget and as your schedule permits, look for a way to nourish your child in ways that school can't, even if it's just talking about a TV program you watched or asking him what he wants to be when he grows up.

Gifts Celebrate the Individual

Rewards celebrate behavior; gifts celebrate the person for who they are, for just—being. As you read in Chapter 2, gifts are more important to some people than others. Gifts are given to celebrate

73

an event, like a birthday, or a milestone, like a graduation. They are typically more expensive and more significant than the "peanuts" you use as rewards.

Gifts do *not* change behavior. Your child won't stop biting you if you buy him a bike for his birthday anymore than you'll change your behavior if your partner buys you a dozen roses to butter you up. That's why you can't withhold gifts on Christmas if your child misbehaves in December, no matter what the stories say about lumps of coal in stockings for "bad" kids. Withholding Christmas or birthday presents because of misbehavior can deeply hurt a child by failing to celebrate him for who he is, imperfections and all.

Bribes: A Bad Deal

A caregiver who feels like nothing he does can improve his child's behavior might turn to bribes out of desperation. Bribes do *not* change behavior and can be a dangerous path to start down. In contrast to rewards, bribes are offered on the spur of the moment, and can have short-term effects, but the trade off is more, worse defiance in the long run. Also, bribes tend to escalate into grandiosity very quickly, and the next thing you know, you're offering your child $500 if he'll just get *one lousy A.*

Once you start offering bribes, your child will misbehave to watch you squirm and then give him a treat that you hadn't even considered. Here's how it works: You take your child to a department store. Your child begins grand-scale misbehavior: pulling items off of shelves, screaming at the top of his lungs, throwing himself down in the middle of a busy aisle, and otherwise humiliating you and making it impossible to get your shopping done. If you start furtively whispering bribes—"If you just get up and be quiet, we'll go buy you a toy from the toy store"—you've just painted yourself into a corner and simultaneously taught your child to act up again next time you go to a department store. As your child gets more daring and skilled, you'll be faced with escalating taunts like, "So what will you give me if I *don't* knock all these mannequins over?"

Reinforcing Emotional Bonds

Ideally, you want to use rewards as a bonding experience. You can bond over your child's growth and progress, over her excitement about the rewards, and over an increased awareness of what she likes and what motivates her—all key to helping her take the million baby steps on the way to a thriving adulthood.

Rewards That Create Bonds

One-on-one time with a parent, especially for young children, can be a huge reward. If your child's behavior has become so disruptive that you haven't spent any time together except to try to correct behavior, she could probably use some positive time with you.

 Essential

Bonds come not just from the warm and fuzzy activities outlined in Chapter 2—which are a good place to start—but from the trust that another person will be there for you, and that you can count on her to be fair, honest, and by your side through thick and thin.

Using a point system with options for different rewards like "Read a book with Mom in the middle of the day," or "Go on a picnic with Dad" can strengthen your bonds and give your child the ability to squeeze in some extra "five-minute freezes" that you otherwise wouldn't make time for.

Rewards That Foster Independence

Conversely, your child needs the opportunity to establish her own identity, one that's separate from you and your family. The older a child, the more important this becomes, and your expression of love is one of gracefully allowing the bird space to flap its wings. At the same time, you don't just let the bird leave for good on its first venture out of the nest.

Rewards that foster independence are *extremely* effective with older children. Extended phone privileges and curfews work well to motivate compliance with rules, as do privileges to join extracurricular activities, or time to pursue outside interests and hobbies. It may be painful to watch your child grow without you there in person, but your child needs you to be her parent, not her friend, and not necessarily her companion for life. If you are steady in your support, you'll give your child the courage to move forward and the protection to fall back on you when she makes mistakes.

CHAPTER 6

Rules and Consequences

You may have a pretty good idea already of the rules and consequences you want in your home. If your child's behavior has gotten out of control, pick just a few of the most important rules to think about and focus on as you read this chapter. Start small. It's important that you do not harp on rules or use the strategies in this chapter until you have implemented the praise discussed in Chapter 5.

How Kids and Teens Interpret Rules and Consequences

Despite everything your child says and does to the contrary, *she wants rules and consequences.* Children need to know where the boundaries are because they know instinctively that they need adult protection to survive. Without you to show her what's safe and what's not, what's acceptable and what's not, your child could get hurt. Her behavior is not a demand for no rules; it's a demand that you stick to them.

Laissez-faire Parenting

In the last fifty years, a laid-back approach to parenting has become somewhat popular. *Laissez-faire* (pronounced "lay-say fair") is a French term that translates roughly as "letting people do whatever they want." It's a style of economic policy that says governments should not interfere with economics, and just let the marketplace play out as it will. Letting your children do whatever they want, or "laissez-faire parenting," is *not* effective at shaping your child's behavior.

As people have grown more aware of the dangers of child abuse and of the power of praising positive behavior, enforcement of rules and consequences has fallen by the wayside or been dismissed as "too harsh." That's a simplification of how to effectively shape behavior—you need to use both the positive and negative sides of the coin. Laissez-faire parenting is not only ineffective, it can be harmful because it leaves children open to danger and leaves parents and other people stressed by inappropriate, defiant, or violent behaviors that go unchecked. Moreover, while inappropriate behavior can sometimes bring about its own natural consequence, relying exclusively for behavioral reinforcement on natural consequences is problematic because they can be serious, delayed, or ineffectual.

For example, if your child is about to touch a rosebush after you've told her fifty times not to because she might prick her finger, allowing the consequence to play out naturally can be effective because it's immediately uncomfortable (ouch!) and directly affects her. On the other hand, allowing her to skip her homework by reasoning that she'll suffer by not qualifying for a good job in the future if she doesn't get good grades now, imposes too serious a consequence that is too delayed to be effective. Also, allowing a kid to steal the neighbor's bike because she'll have to learn that other people won't like her if she steals from them won't be effective—if your child doesn't empathize with other people, she may not care how her actions affect others.

Kids Want Limits

Kids want limits. They even ask for them. It's called "testing" or "challenging," and it's very trying for the parents. If you think back to when your child was first learning to walk, you can see the very beginning of this behavior. If you told her not to pull on the plant in the living room because you didn't want it to fall on her, or simply didn't want it shredded to bits, you might recall that she stopped. For a second. *And then she looked right at you and grabbed the plant again.* "You gonna stop me?" that look said. "Isn't this the limit? Isn't this what you just told me *not* to do? So what are you going to do about it?" That, in a nutshell, is exactly how kids ask for limits and challenge you to enforce them. It's how they test whether you care about them enough to step in and stop them. Kids view your enforcement of rules as an act of love.

 Alert

Kids will "try on" all types of behaviors to see your reaction. You might be at a loss for where your six-year-old daughter heard a particular swear word, but save the detective work ("Who taught you to talk like that?") for later. When you're with her, focus instead on the rule: "That's swearing. We don't use that word in our house."

Kids don't ask you to enforce rules in so many words because they're not capable—it all works on an instinctual level. Testing you allows you the opportunity to answer your child's question: "Do you care enough about me to protect me from what you've told me is harmful?" You'll have to answer "yes" several times for all the major rules in order to prove to your child that you back up what you say.

When Kids Win

If you don't step in and enforce the rules, your child will feel unloved, unsafe, and unparented. You have to be stronger than she is and send her the message that you can protect her and will shelter her from whatever harm the world throws her way. Looking the other way seems, at first glance, the easier option: wouldn't it be easier, just for today, to let your kid play videogames when she's supposed to be doing her homework so you can get dinner ready without interruption for once? But looking the other way when rules are broken is a slippery slope, because your child will repeat the behavior and try something else to see if that's negotiable, too. In the long run, letting today's rule be broken is actually harder for you, because you have to deal with twice the rule-breaking tomorrow.

Unfortunately, if you let defiant behaviors slide, they will escalate as your child cries out for your help. "How far can I go before somebody stops me?" is the rough translation of these behaviors. That's another reason why threats of suicide or homicide should be taken extremely seriously—it's the kid's last card. That's the worst she can do, and if she threatens to do it and you don't react, you've essentially sent her a message that says, "Go for it. I don't care about you or anything you do."

How to Set Rules

Again, start small. If your child has been displaying defiant behavior, take all of the nit-picky rules off the table for now and focus on a few rules that can increase the safety and peace in your home. You're not letting the other behaviors slide, you're taking a systematic approach to effective enforcement that's going to take a few weeks or months to round out.

Forming Most Important Rules

Divide the rules you'd like to see in your home into three categories: very important, less important, and negotiable. To do this, make a list of all of the problem behaviors that you think need correcting. Next, put a checkmark next to the three behaviors you think are most problematic. Alone or with your partner, form a "Most Important Rules" list using no more than three checked behaviors from your list. Some appropriate rules for the "Most Important" list could be:

- Always tell an adult before you leave the house.
- Go to school every day.
- No putting holes in walls or windows.
- No harming the pet.
- Complete and turn in homework every day.
- Bedtime is 9:00 P.M. Go to bed on time every night.
- No hitting.
- Weapons are not allowed in the house.

The rules you choose should be age-appropriate and based on a problem you currently have. So, if you don't have a problem with destruction of property, a rule against putting holes in the walls is not only unnecessary, it could backfire by showing an already defiant kid where he can find another button to push on your already overloaded control panel. These will be the basic, non-negotiable rules for your household from this day forward, no exceptions. Write the list down, but don't announce it yet, because there are a few more steps to this process.

Forming Less Important Rules

Take another look at your list. Now that you've clarified your priorities, choose three to five more behaviors that you'd like to see corrected later, after your child has a handle on obeying the top three rules. These are behaviors that are certainly disruptive, but that you can live with for a few more weeks because they don't directly harm you, your child, or anybody else in the house. Make a list of three to five new, less important rules based on this list. The rules should be specific to behaviors, not general or attitude-oriented. Some examples could be:

- No swearing.
- No yelling closer than two feet from another person's face.
- Curfew is 6:00 P.M. on school nights and 9:00 P.M. on Fridays, Saturdays, and the day before a holiday.

- No friends in the house unless an adult is home.
- Keep a parent in your sight at all times in public places.
- Maximum two hours of (TV, computer, videogames) per day.

These will be non-negotiable at a later date. Writing them down now can give you comfort because you can get some peace from knowing they *will* be resolved soon. But for now, put a star next to these and save them for later. You will also create a third set of rules that you negotiate with your child after that.

How Kids and Teens Interpret Consequences

A rule without a consequence has no more meaning than the law without a law enforcement system—it's just a bunch of meaningless words that, no matter, how kindly or firmly you state them, translate as "Blah, blah, blah." If you don't put your consequences in place, your child will roll her eyes and walk all over you, and you'll get sick of repeating the rules.

Kids Want Consequences

Kids hate consequences, but they want them. It's the consequence that shows you're serious about the rules. When a kid breaks a rule to test you, they're testing to see what you'll *do*. You have to take action with a consequence. Like the baby playing with the potted plant in the living room, a kid who breaks the rules is essentially saying, "You gonna stop me?" Your answer must be yes.

 Essential

Unless a diagnosis of cognitive delays or learning disabilities has been made, assume your child is smart enough to understand the relation between rules and consequences. Don't get bogged down or delayed by wondering if setting up consequences is too sudden or illogical.

The consequences you set up must be effective at stopping the unwanted behavior. If you choose a consequence that's negligible to your child—the proverbial "slap on the wrist"—it won't be effective. The trick is to be in touch with your child enough through your bonding experiences to know what types of consequences will be most effective.

Why Kids Fight Consequences

Kids will fight consequences when you've done a good job of selecting consequences they hate. That means you're being effective! If your child loves videogames, "no videogames for three days" is effective; if she is embarrassed easily in front of her friends, "mom attends school with you for a day to keep an eye on you" could work at getting her to stay in school all day and behave herself while there.

The problem is that many times parents choose consequences that are easy on themselves. Many adults are loathe to take away stimulating, fun activities, because those activities make it easy on the caregiver to cook, clean, and attend to other business. Simply put, if playing with the neighbors or watching DVDs gets the kid out of your hair long enough to pay the bills, it's not attractive to ground him. But you might have to.

Selecting Consequences

Some consequences are more effective than others. Fortunately, today there's a great deal of scientific evidence to back up behavior modification strategies. What's outlined here are those methods proven to work in clinical treatment settings and in homes just like yours.

What's Effective

In order for a consequence to be effective, it must be:

- Immediate
- Age-appropriate

- Unpleasant for your child
- A good match for the crime
- Not too long—kids will give up if punishment stretches out into oblivion
- Not negotiable after the rule has been broken

Consequences that are effective can largely be grouped into two categories: removals and impositions. A "removal" is taking something away from the child, such as your attention, an exciting environment, or a pleasant activity. The most well-known and widely used removal is time out. Other effective removals are:

- Grounding your child from social activities for a weekend
- Taking away screen time for a day
- Immediately leaving play group, the park, a friend's house, a party, or Grandma and Grandpa's house if the child is not behaving there
- Taking away a cell phone or electronic device for one to three days
- No dessert that night
- Forfeiting a turn to choose an outing or choose what's for dinner

Impositions, on the other hand, are consequences that impose some new situation on the child. Paying a fine, having Mom accompany the youngster to school for a day, pulling weeds or doing other extra chores, having to run errands with Dad because the youngster can't be left at home alone—these are impositions. If you're thinking that effective strategies require a lot of your time and energy to enforce, you're right.

What's Not Effective

Corporal punishment—very hard spankings, hitting, restraint, and other punishments causing physical discomfort—is not usually effective, and most of them are child abuse or border on it. You should know that hitting a child with an object, including a belt, is generally considered child abuse and that belt spankings have landed more than one adult in a correctional facility in the last few years. Corporal punishment is also problematic because it tends to escalate—if your kid doesn't do what you want, and your method of discipline is spanking, what happens if he still doesn't cooperate after a spanking? Do you spank him again? Harder? With something else? If that was your only strategy, before you knew it, you'd be committing child abuse. With a defiant child, corporal punishment could escalate into an all-out fistfight with you getting hurt yourself.

 Alert

> If you feel you have no avenues for effective discipline other than corporal punishment, then it's advisable to get some input and outside perspective from a qualified therapist. There are many more effective ways to get your child to cooperate than spankings, and a therapist can help you form habits for doing so if you're having trouble on your own.

Also ineffective are punishments that make the child feel bad about himself. These usually take the form of some subtle bashing, like telling a child you don't like him when he misbehaves, or being sarcastic. Comments like "I don't like tattletales," "You're bad," or "Get out of my sight," don't send a message of unconditional love. Sarcasm such as "Well, well, I see someone *finally* decided to stop that obnoxious whining," is not a great example of family cooperation and kindness. Humiliation, such as punishing a child publicly, also won't get what you want; the kid won't be receptive to the message you're trying to send if shame is at the forefront of his emotions.

Also, warnings are ineffective. "You're cruisin' for a bruisin'," "I've just about had it with you," and "If you do that one more time," are cliché warnings that don't work because your child interprets them as, "Hey, cool! I get to break the rule one more time— maybe more!" You don't need to warn your child that you're going to enforce the rules; you just do. And finally, empty threats such as "I'll break your neck" may sound impressive, but since you're not actually going to do it, and your child knows this, he will completely disregard what you're saying.

Match Consequences to Behaviors

The punishment should fit the crime, as the saying goes. Take out your list of "Most Important Rules" and put an effective consequence (a removal or an imposition) next to each one. Because these are the most important rules in your house, the consequences should be fairly stiff. Finally, clearly number and write the rules and their respective consequences on a large sheet of paper in the following format:

- Go to school every day. If you skip school or leave school, I will go with you to school the next day, or as soon as I can get off work, and be by your side all day long.
- No putting holes in walls or windows. If you do, you will spend the next weekend fixing the holes instead of going to any social activities.
- No pulling the cat's tail. If you do, you will not be allowed to play with the cat for two days and will be grounded the next weekend.
- Complete and turn in homework every day. If you do not, I will go with you to school the next day, or as soon as I can get off work, and be by your side all day long.
- Bedtime is 9:00 P.M. Go to bed on time every night. If you do not, you will skip your extracurricular activities the next day (or the next time you have one).

- No hitting. If you hit anyone, you will sit in time out for five minutes.
- Weapons are not allowed in the house. If I think you have one, I will call the police.

 Essential

For the time being, go with a practical approach and don't try to set up rules if you'll have no idea whether your child has complied. If you're working when your child comes home, you won't know if your child is watching TV instead of doing homework, so frame the rule based on what you can measure: completed homework.

Now you have a clear list of rules and their consequences—consequences that are fitting and effective. It's time to introduce them to your child.

Time to Talk to Your Child

In a moment of downtime when you don't anticipate an immediate power struggle (don't wait too long), approach your child and say, "I love you too much to let things go on like they have been, and it is my job to keep you safe and help you grow up with every advantage in life, so I am laying down some new rules. These are the three basic rules in our house, and the consequences for not obeying them." Show the child your list. If your child is younger, read it to him; if he's older, have him read it himself.

Ask if there are any questions, or if there is anything that isn't clear, but don't ask your child to grant you permission to lay down the rules by ending sentences with "Okay?" *You're* in control. You might get questions like, "What if I just hurt the dog a little bit?" and you should answer that breaking a rule just a little bit is still breaking a rule. Tell your child that the new rules are in effect immediately. Then tell your child you love him, and end the conversation.

Post the rules in a conspicuous place, and expect him to begin testing them right away.

When a Rule Is Broken

When a rule is broken—and they will be broken—you must be prepared. Don't wait until a rule is broken to think about how you'll handle enforcing it. Give some time and thought to how you'll enforce rules if your child breaks one at the supermarket, in the car, while you're busy, in front of company, or at someone else's house.

React Immediately

No matter where you are or what you're doing, react immediately when your child violates one of your three most important rules. Allowing defiance of the rules for a few minutes until you're done paying the bills or cooking dinner shows your child that paying the bills and cooking dinner are more important than she is. In order to stop defiant behavior, you'll need to make it a priority for a little while.

When a rule is broken, immediately say, "No. That is against the rules," and immediately state the consequence from the list, such as "No soccer tomorrow" or "Go sit in time out." Your child will whine, or maybe try to kick, hit, or let loose with swear words. Don't engage in a discussion, and don't respond to the outcry; unless your child is hurting someone, go back to whatever you were doing.

If your child breaks another rule as part of her protest, say, "No. That is against the rules," and immediately state the corresponding consequence from the list. Don't back down or allow good behavior or apologies to erase the consequence. Ignore all other defiant behaviors at this point in time, such as a child sticking out her tongue at you or saying she hates you, and focus on the three major rules in your home.

Forming the Less Important Rules

Take heart—you'll have more than just three rules in your house. Revisit your rule list and look at the items you marked with a star, the "Less Important Rules." Has anything new come forward that you think is more important than what you've written down? Have you decided that you can live without something in the "Less Important" category? If so, it's okay to make changes now, before you add these rules.

Adding Consequences

As you did with the Most Important Rule list, select consequences that are age-appropriate, effective, and match the crime. Several consequences that you've been using for violations of the most important rules may still apply; you may not choose accompanying your child to school for something on this list, but you probably will still find time out, loss of screen time, and grounding effective.

 Alert

Enforce these rules just as diligently as you did the Most Important Rules. Just because they're less important doesn't mean they're up for debate. All it means is that you're breaking this process into a few manageable steps instead of overwhelming your family with too many changes, which would likely result in more defiance.

Once you have selected the consequences, write them out clearly as you did the first time. Your list may sound like this: "No yelling within two feet of another person's face. If you do, you will sit in the hallway for fifteen minutes," or "Be home by 5:00 on school nights and 9:00 on Fridays, Saturdays, and the day before a holiday. If you're late even one minute, you are grounded the next Friday or Saturday."

When to Announce Them

Your child is ready for the new batch of rules when he has been complying steadily with the first batch for awhile. For some kids, that's a few days, for others, a couple of weeks. It's probably longer for kids with more severe defiance. What's more important than a specific measure of time is that your child's behavior has become a habit. If your child is automatically obeying the first batch of rules and you are using the consequences much, much less, then you're ready . . . as long as you have been regularly rewarding and praising these positive behaviors. If you haven't, you need to develop that habit as well, or your child will resist the new rules—it will seem like nothing's ever good enough for you, so he might as well give up now.

Once you think your child is ready, prime the pump before talking about new rules. Casually mention that you're so proud of how he's been doing with X and Y, and that you're thinking it might be time to talk about making changes to Z. That gives him a heads-up that there'll be another conversation soon. Next, choose a calm moment and show him the new list. Say, "There are some things you're doing that are disruptive to our family and can work against you in the long run. I love you and our family too much to let them continue. Here are some new rules to stop those disruptive and harmful behaviors." Read the child the list, or have an older child read it himself. Offer to answer any questions, and post the list in a conspicuous place. Tell your child that after he makes a habit of complying with these rules, he'll be able to help you write the rules next time around. Expect your child to test these rules and perhaps even relapse for a few days. Just be patient and stick to your plan.

Forming the Negotiable Rules

Once your child has made a habit of following all of the rules, and you have regularly rewarded her compliance, revisit your original list and look at what you have left. If there are more than about five behaviors you'd like to change, prioritize them or group them so you have five or fewer. Rewrite these behaviors on a fresh piece of paper and approach your child during a calm moment. Initiate a conversation that starts off with praise, like, "I've noticed your behavior has improved dramatically in the last few weeks/months. I know it hasn't been easy. You've done an awesome job and I'm really proud of you."

 Essential

> Uncomfortable silences are a necessary part of a true dialogue. If you really want to solicit someone's input, allow five to ten seconds for the person to respond. It can seem like a long time if you're tense, so try counting in your head before you speak again.

Allow your child to respond, and don't take the bait if she rolls her eyes or finds something sarcastic to say. Let your praise remain. Next, tell your child that there are a few more behaviors that are disruptive and could harm her and your family in the long run, but she has earned the chance to work with you to decide how to implement new rules and what the consequences will be for not complying with them. Show the child the list.

At this point, your desired rules may address neatness, organization, keeping up appearances, or planning for the future. It's time to be flexible. Ask your child what she thinks of the proposed rules, and if she doesn't respond after ten seconds, ask if she thinks they're fair as is, or if she would like this chance to make changes before the rules are set. If your child seems hesitant, offer to let her think about it for a day and set a time within twenty-four hours to finalize the rules. At the agreed-upon time, if your child still doesn't engage, implement the rules as is according to the steps for the Less Important Rules.

If your child is willing to engage with you, ask her what she thinks is fair. Be willing to negotiate and compromise—flexibility is one thing you want from your child, and this is your chance to model it!

Some compromises may include agreeing to eat dinner as a family twice a week instead of every day, picking up toys in the living room every night but letting the bedroom go for a week or more at a time, or setting curfew at 10:00 P.M. on weekends instead of 9:00 P.M. You're not looking for perfection, you're looking for a deal you can live with that leaves both of you feeling, if not great, at least satisfied.

Finally, work on the consequences. Ask your child if she thinks the same types of consequences you've used so far would keep her from breaking the rules, or if she has something new to offer. If she won't engage, ask her to tell you what she hates and would really, really not want to do if she broke a rule. If she doesn't say anything, give an exaggerated guess, like, "How about no TV for two weeks?" She may jump in and counter with, "No TV for one week." That is a great compromise, so take her up on it.

On the other hand, if your child says, "I should get a gallon of ice cream," say, "I think that wouldn't get you to obey the rule. We should stick with the consequences we've been using, like grounding you for a weekend" and see if that gets her to speak up. If nothing you say results in a dialogue, implement the consequences you think fit as described for the Less Important Rules, and tell your child she'll get another chance to help with rule development in a few weeks or months. Once your rules are set, write them down and post them, and don't negotiate on them again.

When to Stop

It's time to stop adding batches of rules when you feel calmer and you think your child's behavior has improved to the point where it's no longer a constant disruption to your home, your family, the school, and any other environments where your child is regularly. Once you are into a cycle of regular bonding, praise, and rewards, you'll need fewer rules because you'll talk with your child more often and have a chance to nurture your child's sense of right and wrong. However, every once in awhile, you will need to add a new rule to the list—just use the same format for writing them down and solicit your child's input if you think it is a circumstance that would benefit from negotiation.

Rules for Public Places

You've probably gotten to the point where you dread going to the supermarket with a defiant kid in tow. It's hard to implement consequences in public, and it's also downright embarrassing.

Don't wait until you're in the situation to figure out what you'll do. Just as you do with your other rules, you'll need to give this some thought beforehand and tell your child what the rules are *before* you go inside the store or walk into your friend's house. A quick, clear explanation suffices: "Stay where you can see me at all times and don't take anything off the shelves," or "Keep your hands to yourself and sit down during the meal."

If your child doesn't comply, you can do one of two things: implement a time out, or with fun environments like birthday parties if you don't need to be there for your own or a sibling's sake, you can simply leave.

Allowing Freedom

The function of rules is to keep your child and other family members safe, your house in one piece, and, to some extent, to provide the structure and predictability necessary to create a calm environment that allows him to grow and thrive. To that end, it's not desirable to have rules for every situation—if you veer toward extreme structure, you risk thwarting your child's independence, ability to deal with new situations, and ability for self-expression.

Once you have a handle on safety, basic neatness, and standard etiquette, you'll probably enjoy a lot more peace in your home. Don't implement new rules until new situations warrant them, and solicit your child's input whenever possible, especially as he grows older. As the months pass, you'll get to know your child better, and might find even new things to appreciate and love about him.

CHAPTER 7

Consistency

The importance of consistency when working with a defiant child cannot be over-emphasized. It's the most essential requirement in disciplining effectively. It's important to understand how consistency helps kids, how to help other adults to be consistent, and how to hang in there long-term.

How Kids and Teens Respond to Consistency

No matter how well you've selected your rules, how much you praise your kids, or how effectively you discipline them, you must be consistent, or your efforts will be in vain and your household will still be in crisis. Kids need consistency to get the message because your actions speak louder than your words—it's part of how they're wired.

How Habits Work

Riding a bike is a cliché example of how habits are formed. Think back on the first time you rode a bike, and how difficult and scary it was. Yet you kept trying, and each time, it was a little easier. The more you did it, the easier it became. In fact, after a few days, you probably couldn't even imagine *not* knowing how to do it! The same holds true with each new endeavor.

Strange as it may seem, all of this has to do with how the brain grows and functions, and it is in children that its growth and function is most marked and amazing. To boil down decades of research into a sentence: brain cells only grow when they are stimulated. Brain cells grow and are strengthened by use; like muscles, using them makes them get bigger. That's the simple reason why practicing makes it easier to do something.

What's more, brain cells don't grow at the same pace or in the same way during a person's life. If you fail to provide enrichment for certain activities during the critical period of time in which the brain wants to work on them, your child's efficient brain will trim those cells or use them for other purposes; or, they'll just fail to grow larger. Language learning, for example, must take place during childhood, or your brain "turns off" the function for learning it, which is why kids can learn languages so much more easily than adults can. Is it impossible to learn a foreign language as an adult? No, but it is much, much more difficult, and very few adults will attain native-like fluency.

Sticking with a new endeavor is what makes it become a habit, and the sooner you start, the easier it will be for both you and your child. What's going on around your child strongly impacts the development of his brain. In order for your child's brain cells to learn the new rewards, rules, and consequences, and to behave accordingly in a way that becomes automatic, you must remain consistent while his brain develops.

Benefits of Consistency

In the emotional realm, consistency makes kids feel safe: when they know what to expect, they feel secure. Clear rules, clear consequences, pleasant rewards, and the knowledge you can count on them like you count on the sun rising each day—this makes a kid feel secure, safe, and stable. Only then can he maximize his potential. In addition, your child will be a better student and future employee when discipline is consistent. Consistency means not only consistent discipline on an individual basis, but from child to child and from parent to parent.

When rewards, rules, and consequences are consistent, kids think, "Okay, I know what to expect. I may not like the rules, but I know they're fair and that I'm not being singled out, and I know what will happen if I *don't* follow them." After a few tastes of consistently applied discipline, most kids will choose to follow the rules, which are set up for their well-being anyway. They know they can rely on their parents and trust that their needs will be met. So consistency makes for a happy, relaxed kid!

 Alert

> Without consistency, a child feels his world is in flux and he may grow anxious and more defiant. In addition, he'll need to test the rules much more to see if you really mean what you say. Obviously, that can wear you down in a hurry. Consistency has the added benefit of making your life a little easier.

Think back to the experience of learning to ride a bike—if it became easier over time, you can also conclude that the beginning was the toughest part. Take the courage to start now and trust that the beginning is a "hump" you need to work hard to pedal over before you can start coasting.

Consistency Between Two Married Parents

Perhaps you're wondering if part of your child's behavior problems could stem from inconsistent parenting by you and your partner. Children don't distinguish well between "Mom's Rules" and "Dad's Rules." Not knowing what to expect from parent to parent can also lead to anxiety and further defiant behaviors. In order to help your child comply with "Our Rules," you'll need to enlist your partner.

Having an Initial Conversation

In most families, one parent shoulders more childrearing responsibilities than the other. Still, it's important that you share your observations, insights, and recommendations using effective communication skills in order to help your child; if not, your child will get inconsistent messages and may even enjoy playing the two of you against each other.

First, make time for an initial conversation. You and your partner may have little downtime—how you spend what you have is up to you. It's extremely important that you and your partner be on the same page, so you need to have a conversation—or several—in order to best co-parent and take action as a united front.

For the greatest chance of success, use the communication skills taught at the beginning of Chapter 8. Try to approach the situation from a place of common ground: "I think we're both concerned about Zoe's behavior. I have some thoughts and have read some material I think might be helpful," is a good opener. Be prepared that your partner may need to vent before you can continue. He might say something like, "You're darn right! Do you know what she said to me the other day? All I told her to do was to pick up her socks, and the next thing I know, it's an all-out battle. . . ." If so, be patient, listen, and then respond by recognizing your partner's emotions before rattling off advice: "Are you feeling frustrated because Zoe had a temper tantrum over something that seemed inconsequential to you?" You may need to go through a few rounds of venting and listening empathetically before you can move on.

When you can move on, repeat that you have some ideas and observations. If you must be extremely concise, say, "I've read a lot of material that's helped me understand Zoe's behavior, what might be causing it, and how best to start fixing it. You can read it, too, or I can give you the synopsis. If you want the synopsis, or can't make time to read about defiant behavior soon, I'd like you to trust me to guide us on managing Zoe's behavior. In order to be effective at making our home more peaceful, it's extremely important that we are united in our plan of action. Here is what I think is causing the defiant behavior, and here's how I think we can start to fix it."

 Alert

> When you outline your recommendations, be sure to point out that you are recommending a new approach because the problem has been going on a long while and your current methods of discipline aren't working. Otherwise, a stressed-out partner is likely to throw his hands up in defeat, or conversely, state that harsher discipline is needed.

If your partner will not get on board with you, or agrees but doesn't follow through, suggest that your inability to co-parent could be a factor in your child's behavior, and suggest marital counseling to help the two of you communicate more effectively. If your partner is still resistant, seek out counseling for yourself because you will need extra support to help your child if you are going to go it alone.

Daily Dealing

Once you have your partner on board, everyone should know what to expect. When a rule is broken, consequences must be applied immediately, or immediately after a parent finds out. Here's something very important: *doling out consequences is the responsibility of the parent who is in charge at the moment.* Don't let behaviors slide until your partner comes downstairs and stops them, or imply that doom comes when the other parent gets home by saying things like, "You're going to be in big trouble when Dad comes home!" All this does is divide you and your partner and make the one who won't enforce rules look weak to your child. It puts a strain on your marriage and gives your kid the opportunity to play you off of one another.

Of course, your child will test your power. She'll test the rules, and test each parent individually and as a team. Especially if your child is older and accustomed to inconsistency, you may have to stick with it for quite awhile before she gets the message (and her brain, too, which has developed in an inconsistent environment). At the end of each day, when you and your partner have time to relax, you can do a five-minute review of what happened during the day, how you felt about it, and how to stay strong for the next day. If you're pressed for time or your partner is distracted, give your partner the headlines rather than the play-by-play.

 Question

What about your feelings?
Your feelings about what's happened during the day can get lost when you're keeping your partner up to speed. If so, try saying something like, "Today ended up okay. I just want to tell you about it because I feel like I need to vent and want some comfort so I can be strong for tomorrow."

If something unforeseen happens, you might need to talk to your partner ("But *Dad* told me I could wear this to school!" "Well, *Mom* always lets us ride our bikes across that street!"). First, think about the rules you've made and if they apply to the situation, and do what you think is best in the moment. Talk to your partner when your child can't see or hear you. Don't discuss new rules and their enforcement right in front of your child if you think the two of you might disagree. All disagreements about rules should be resolved when your child is out of earshot; otherwise, your child will look for the cracks in your foundation where she can lodge herself and try to make a bigger fissure.

Consistency Between Divorced Parents

If you and the other parent are divorced or otherwise separated, chances are you'll have a much tougher time with consistency. After all, if you're divorced, you probably have pretty different values and may not be friendly or even be able to talk to each other.

Doing Your Best

If you're one of the lucky divorced parents who can have a peaceful conversation with an ex, try having an initial conversation as described above. Then, ask your ex if she has any concerns or observations to contribute. Hopefully, you're both aware of major issues already.

Next, show your ex the list of rewards, rules, and consequences you've devised for your own home. Say, "I want to share with you the rewards, rules, and consequences that I've set up for my house. They might work for you, or they might not. If you think they would, or if you think we could make similar rules for both of our houses, it would probably go a long way to helping solve this behavior problem and making both our lives easier. You can get back to me later if you want." Allow your ex time to think about this instead of forcing an answer on the spot.

If you think your ex will resist working with you, enlist the help of a third party, such as a child psychologist, who can serve as a go-between and point of balance so that neither parent feels the other is trying to gain control over the situation. You can each work on a list of rules separately with a psychologist and finalize a finished product that satisfies everyone.

Finally, if your ex won't join in with a third party, you may have to go it alone. You will probably benefit from regular meetings with a psychologist who can support and guide you. Don't despair—your child will learn that *you* can be consistent, and that you care enough to do whatever is in your power to help him. It may take longer, but with time your own consistency will develop its own power, and your child will gain increased trust in you.

Other Authorities

In order to maintain consistency between the rewards, rules, and consequences of your home and those of your child's other environments—school, after-care, Grandma's house, the world in general—you'll need to explain to your child the variations on a theme that are at play. It's important to recognize the authority of the rest of the world holds over your child's life because, remember, your child is strongly influenced by it.

The Themes

If you think about it, most rules are variations on a few themes:

- Not harming other people and their property (no hitting, no throwing balls in the house, and waiting for the light to turn green before you proceed, are examples)
- Fulfilling responsibilities to ensure the individual and the group survive and thrive (washing the dishes, doing homework, not littering, and so on)
- Trusting others to do the same (obeying your parents and the principal, sharing, using manners, not taking the biggest piece of pie, etc.)

For young children, and older children who may need some extra guidance, it helps to have an explicit conversation—and several that build on it afterward—about how rules are formed and why we give certain people authority to set them. Introduce the basic concepts above, and whenever there's a question about a rule in another environment, you can refer to these concepts. You can say something such as, "I think when your teacher says running in the classroom is against the rules, she's showing she cares about your safety and the safety of the other kids. That is one of those rules about not hurting people. You see, the classroom is a small space, and there's a lot of stuff you could trip on and people you could run into, so if you run there, you or another kid could get badly hurt." When your child is ready, you can explain that laws are rules that lots of people have agreed on.

 Essential

This is a fitting time to explain democracy, voting, and leadership. A child who loves attention may be keen on the idea of being a leader to others. Steer your child's attention in the direction of leaders you admire, and explain what makes them successful. Ironically, it's often selflessness.

You might also refer to the Golden Rule, which appears in many places, including the Bible and most religions. The gist of most translations is, "Treat other people the way you'd want them to treat you." You can also use Dr. Kathy's Golden Rule, "Act in ways that make you feel good about yourself and proud of your behavior."

The Authorities

Later, your child will undoubtedly want to know just what makes the teacher or another authority the boss. "Why can't *I* set the rules?" she might wonder. "Why can't *you* go to the school and make them reverse my detention?" If so, it's time to explain that authority isn't just deemed, it's earned.

You can say something such as, "That does sound very frustrating. I trust the teacher to set rules and consequences for your classroom. She's been doing this for awhile. First, she studied how to teach in university, and then, the school picked her over a lot of other teachers they could have hired instead, and she's taught hundreds of kids, so I have to trust that she knows how to handle this best." Showing that an authority has fulfilled some criteria instead of being randomly handed a crown is helpful.

 Alert

> Your rules and consequences should be consistent with the local law, and so should your own behavior. If using firecrackers is against the law, but you let your kids do it anyway because it's a holiday, you've taught them to disrespect the law whenever they decide it is appropriate.

It's also helpful to explain division of labor. A child who has a high level of anxiety may be looking for an explanation along these lines: "Everybody has to work together. No one person can do *everything*, so each person chooses a specialty that works for him or her. We have to trust that firefighters know how to fight fires, doctors know how to keep us healthy, mechanics will fix our cars, and teachers know how to teach. We have to trust that our family members have our best interests at heart. Is the system perfect? Do people we trust always have our best interests at heart? No, but it usually works at keeping people safe, healthy, and happy, and I feel safe this way."

Making Habits Last

Does it feel like parenting is a long nightmare that stretches from here until the year 2025 without a break? Are you worried that you might get burned out before your child's habits are really ingrained? If so, you're not alone, but there are several things you can do to strengthen your parenting skills.

Start Now

Consider that the sooner you start forming and reinforcing good habits, the stronger they'll be. Start now! Don't wait until next year, or after the holidays, or until you get through a tough project at work. The sooner you pedal over the "hump," the sooner you can coast.

It's important to see this as a "glass is half full" situation. Remain positive, and take the stance that you can't change the past, but you can take action in the present and change the course your child is on, directing him to a bright future. Don't agonize over what you haven't done, or how many months or years have gone by since your child first started showing signs of defiance. Stay in the now and take action immediately.

Don't Be a Hero

Another way to be consistent over the long-term is by seeking support. Assume that you are the authority on your child *as an individual*, but that other people have more experience dealing with defiant behaviors, troublesome family dynamics, or marital and financial issues. Enlist the help of a therapist or other helping professional who can keep you on track as well as let you vent and talk about what else in your life you can do to get relief.

If a family member or friend says, "I heard you're having a tough time. Let me know if there's anything I can do!" take her up on it. You can say things like, "I'd love a shoulder to lean on. Do you mind if we have coffee on Wednesday before work?" or "Yes, I really need some practical support. There just aren't enough hours in the day. What kinds of things would you like to help with?"

Also, you can gain additional knowledge from parenting books like this one, support groups for parents through a local hospital or church, or tips from a friend or family member you trust who has older children and has been where you are. Admitting you don't know everything and that you need help is healthy and can come as a huge relief. You don't have to go it alone.

Expect Regressions

After you've been sailing smoothly along, and the rewards, rules, and consequences are working as you hoped, be prepared for a regression. Your child may go through a "honeymoon" period in which he finally begins to cooperate more and throw fewer tantrums. Then, suddenly, *boom!* It seems you're right back where you started. What happened?

On one level, it doesn't matter. Remain consistent. So your son hasn't broken the daily homework rule in three months, and then suddenly he does—enforce the consequences just as you would have the first week the rule was in effect.

On another level, it does matter. Think over the day—was there some kind of trigger that set your child off? Try to pinpoint if there was anything out of the ordinary that factored into the defiant behavior. If appropriate, have a dialogue about it with your child. You can say, "Today was a difficult day. Do you want to tell me a little bit about what happened?" Be prepared for a surly response, or a shrug of the shoulders, and say, "If you want to talk about it with me anytime, just let me know. In the meantime, our rules still stand."

Be prepared for an excuse, because your child is likely testing you again. He might just want to know if you're really serious about these rules, or if you'll give up. Excuses like, "My cell phone died," "I forgot my notebook," and "My sister is stupid and she deserved it," don't hold water because your child uses them to absolve himself of responsibility for his actions.

If, on the other hand, you suspect something has really disturbed your child, or that a rule isn't working, you may need to think more about how to cope with change and disruptions.

Coping with Changes and Disruptions

Granted, life doesn't happen in a vacuum. Change is something we can count on to happen—even if you don't anticipate big events in your child's life, just the act of growing older is a small, if nearly imperceptible change. Then, there are the big events like moving from one grade to another, or summer break, which can seem to throw your world into chaos.

Holidays and Special Occasions

Beware: the more leeway you give a child when it comes to keeping routines and following rules, the more incentive you are giving her to try to push those boundaries even further. *Changes from the routine should be rare and should be the exception to the rule.*

For example, it is appropriate to extend bedtime on a few special holidays per year: Christmas Day, Halloween, the night the cousins you haven't seen in a year arrive on a 7:00 P.M. flight. It's not appropriate to extend bedtime for the entire winter break, or the entire week the cousins are in town. In addition, bedtime can't be extended until the kids just pass out from exhaustion.

 Question

What if our life is so hectic we have to make frequent exceptions? If you need to make frequent exceptions, you may need to reevaluate your lifestyle. Children don't enjoy excitement and full calendars as much as grown-ups do; traveling, eating out, and other "metropolitan" activities can be boring and trying for children.

When you want to make an exception to a rule, do so in an organized way, by explaining the exception ahead of time and setting concrete parameters. You can say something like, "Since it's Halloween, you can go to bed at 9:00 instead of 8:00 just for tonight."

Expect that your child will pick up on this "special occasion" exception and want to find a reason for a special occasion every other evening. Be firm, and tell her: "I know we extended curfew last week for a special occasion, but that's not going to happen very often. Two, three times a year, tops. This is the rule." After a few of these back-and-forth exchanges over exceptions to the rule, you will find the consistency of the rules easier than the exceptions and in fact wonder if the exceptions are even worth the grief.

When a Rule Doesn't Work

There are times when rules just don't work. Perhaps your child has grown out of the 8:00 bedtime now that he's twelve. Maybe having him check in with you at work before he goes to a friend's house is interfering with your ability to do your job. It could be that requiring your child to do homework before playing doesn't work as well as letting him blow off steam on his bike for half an hour. The way to tell when a rule doesn't work is when it doesn't produce the desired result (like finished homework and a more peaceful home), and there is a *pattern* of behavior to indicate it doesn't work, not a one-time fluke.

There's a difference between insistence and consistency. If a rule doesn't make sense, or only serves to underscore your role as the authority rather than help the child and your family thrive, you might need to rethink it. Insisting on blind compliance with rules that don't work, are harmful, or don't make sense just because you want to see "good form," doesn't teach your child to think or to respect your authority. Instead, it causes resentment and rebellion.

Chances are, you'll need to adapt a rule rather than ditching it all together. If you notice your child needs some downtime before starting her homework, observe this over a period of a few days or weeks, and then say, "I've noticed you have a hard time sitting still during your homework. Would it help you sit still if you had a chance to play first?" Solicit her input and show you care about her feelings and needs. Then, make the new rule concrete and measurable, and post it as you have with the other rules. It should say something such as, "Homework time begins at 4:30 P.M." The first day or two of a new routine, you can gently remind the child of the change in the rule, however, if it is broken, you should enforce the consequences as you normally would to show that you aren't being inconsistent; just flexible.

CHAPTER 8

Good Influences

A loving structure in your home is a great start. But once you have cemented some basic good habits to build love and trust, there are more proactive things you can do to grease the parenting wheels and enrich your child's life. Self-realization and an all-around enriching environment help your child be the best she can be.

Communication Skills

Using good communication skills in your home will minimize repetitive fighting and arguing between you and your partner, between you and your child, between siblings, and between your children and the outside world. These skills can be learned, taught, and shared, with surprisingly rewarding results for everyone involved. So why doesn't everyone use them? Two reasons: first, societies have gotten out of the habit; second, it takes courage to communicate skillfully because there's short-term risk involved in caring about others' feelings.

Empathetic Listening

Effective communication begins not with talking, but with listening. It's hard to do when some of your own needs—a shower, a good night's sleep, a few minutes of exercise, financial stability—

are not being met. Try to turn down the white noise in life for a few minutes and really listen to what your child is saying. Isn't it funny that *not* doing anything is the most powerful thing you can do to communicate? But it's true. You have to be present in the moment and receive from your child, without offering advice, trying to solve the problem, launching off into a story about what it was like when you were a kid, or underscoring the life lesson that can be gleaned from the present situation.

To practice empathy, look into the child's eyes as she speaks, nod to encourage her to talk, and, once she's finished, show you've been listening by paraphrasing her words without adding any judgments. For example, if your child comes home and says, "Nobody at school likes me, and I hate them, too," you should say, "It sounds like you're saying nobody at school likes you, and you hate them too." Don't try to replace the word "hate" with "dislike." Your child's feelings are valid and you must find and recognize them to listen empathetically; you can work on her choice of language at another time. Not adding judgments of your own does *not* mean you are stupid or thoughtless in reaction to what your child has said. It simply means you're listening, which is immensely comforting to the child.

Labels versus Actions

When it is your turn to talk, focus on feelings and actions rather than labels. The risk here is that you can only express your own opinions and observations, and cannot be the end-all, be-all authority in the world. To be clear: that does *not* mean you're not in charge of your child and that you can revert to laissez-faire parenting; it means your opinions are your own and you can't foist them on other people. In time, as your children see you treat them with respect and care, they'll grow to think about and respect your opinions rather than swallow them hook, line, and sinker. The advantage to this is that they'll make a habit of doing so and will think about others' opinions in the same way. That will be important when it's time for her to find a life partner: your child needs skills for thinking carefully about others' actions, not a habit of being dominated by whoever comes along and calls herself the queen.

To focus on feelings and actions rather than labels, avoid calling names. Nobody in this world is stupid, ugly, lazy, bad, evil, messy, finicky, or unfocused; neither are they smart, beautiful, hard-working, good, angelic, neat, easy-going, or organized. Those are all judgments, opinions of the speaker or of the family, the media, or general populace. Instead, focus first on actions: "I noticed you cleaned your room three times this week!" "It looks like you don't like broccoli, string beans, or peas, right?" "You've included your brother in your plans to go to the movies." "You've waited to study until the night before your test." These statements focus on the actions you've observed, nothing more.

The "I" Statement

Obviously, your kids need your guidance and input in their lives, and to give them this, you have to speak up and express your point of view. To do so, focus on feelings using "I" statements. "I" statements are commonly taught as a way of communicating effectively and reducing conflict in all human interaction.

 Alert

Choosing the right "feeling words" is crucial. An extensive and extremely helpful list of feeling words can be found in Marshall Rosenberg's *Non-Violent Communication: A Language of Compassion*. The list is divided into words that express how people feel when their needs are being met and how they feel when they aren't.

An "I" statement is a simple expression of your feelings: "I feel *disappointed* because you broke your promise about calling me before you go somewhere." "I feel *sad* when you call me and your brother those names." "I feel *confused* when you tell me you don't like strawberries because you asked me to buy them." "I feel *impatient* when you are not ready on time." "I feel *peaceful* when we hug and talk like this."

Beware using veiled judgments: "I feel you are being lazy" is not an "I" statement of your feelings; it's a judgment of another person. "I feel like you've dropped the ball" is another judgment. Try rephrasing it as "I'm *disappointed* that you only did your homework for three days after our discussion, and haven't done homework at all this week."

Teaching Values

You'll need to think about how kids develop values and identify your own and your partner's core values before you employ specific strategies for teaching them. Your values will guide how you choose subsequent "good influences" for your child.

How Kids Develop Values

Jean Piaget was a Swiss philosopher who did groundbreaking work on child development. One of his theories of child developmental psychology was about "moral education." Piaget's primary argument—controversial at the time—is that kids develop morals by interacting with peers, not because their parents punish them into morality. Like the rest of your child's development, moral development happens in stages as your child gains the capacity for more complex thought.

Piaget and other philosophers have also reasoned that when power is shared between parties rather than having one party dominate the other, children benefit from a real and satisfying intellectual discussion about what's acceptable and ethical in their world, and learn to form their own judgments. This relates directly to the effective communication strategies outlined above—being an effective communicator helps your child develop the morals you desire.

Of course, scarily enough, you can't directly control your child's peer interactions and you have limited control over the environment you live in. Rather than worrying about the troublemakers your kid hangs around with, or wishing you could afford to move to a more peaceful street/school district/city/country/planet where everybody's needs are met and everyone uses "I" statements, focus on what you *can* change.

Values Inventory

What *are* your values, anyway? Do your partner's even match your own? Ask yourself the following questions:

- What is important to you on a physical level?
- What is important to you on an emotional level?
- What is important to you on an intellectual level?
- What is important to you on an interpersonal level?
- What is important to you on a spiritual level?

Make a list of about three to five concepts in each category. For example, everyone needs food, water, and exercise, but we may express those needs differently. One person's list under "Physical" may include "Eat tasty, nutritious food every day and exercise once a week. Wear soft, comfortable clothes." Another's may read, "Eat organic foods and exercise every day." Someone else may write "Keep my blood sugar in check and get a good night's sleep." After you have completed your lists, look for recurring themes.

Ask your partner to do the same, and then compare lists. Do you notice any strong themes, any clusters of ideas? Write them down in the following format: "We value . . . in our family because we want . . . ." Try for three to five core values—more than that can overwhelm your kids—and post them in a conspicuous place or add them to a collective display. Sample core values can be "We value a safe, pleasant home because we want everyone to be comfortable and have the peace they need to grow and thrive," or "We value going to church regularly because we want a relationship with God that gives us inner peace and strength."

Model Your Values

Now the tricky part: modeling your values. If you want your kids to exercise and eat nutritiously, your actions have much, much more weight than your words, so you'll have exercise and eat nutritiously. Sound hard? That's why your kids are fighting it.

You can't request more from them than you can do yourself, or request things that you're completely unwilling to do. Adults are strapped for time by trying to nurture and provide for their kids—ironically, two responsibilities that are so often at odds with each other—but if you don't give your core values importance in your life, you're telling your kids that they're not your core values after all, but lofty, unattainable, and unrealistic ideals.

Extracurricular Activities

That's about all you can do to teach values. The rest is up to the rest of the world, for better or for worse . . . or is it? Okay, so your kids are often surrounded by people with different values than your own. But you can still be a powerful force in making sure your kids pick up appropriate values from their environments.

What Works

Extracurricular activities that teach values effectively are more than just "basketball," "karate," "church camp," and "music lessons." That's the name of what you sign up for, but the activities don't happen in a vacuum—they are "basketball practice every day after school in a competitive league," "karate because all of his friends are in it," "church camp when he's the only boy in his age group," and "music lessons that he hates and that we never asked his input on." As you can see, kids learn more than the basic subject matter or a skill. They also learn how other people value winning and losing, how to be a part of a group, how to sink or swim as an outsider, or that their opinion doesn't really matter because what Dad says, goes.

In order for extracurricular activities to effectively teach values, they must (1) be enriching (not to the exclusion of fun); (2) form a platform for self-realization and/or self-expression; (3) be age-appropriate; and (4) incorporate the child's input. For example, it's common knowledge that music lessons do wonders for kids' cognitive development and build a foundation for healthy self-expression later in life. But if you enroll your kid in music lessons against his will, or the lessons are stiff and over his head, he probably won't get much out of them.

 Fact

> According to TakeLessons, the largest national full-service music lessons company providing students with certified music instructors, parents should look for instructors who balance "hard" skills like experience, education, reputation, and accountability with "soft" skills such as chemistry, excellent listening abilities, and enthusiasm toward the student's musical preferences.

It also helps to challenge your child's values from time to time. Unless your teen really needs the money to get by, consider asking him to volunteer his extra time instead of getting a paying job. There are not many fast-food, retail, or other low-skill jobs that teach life lessons or impart college or career prep knowledge. Ask him instead to volunteer for a cause he's passionate about, like helping at an animal shelter.

What Doesn't Work

Commonly, the worst choice isn't which activity to choose, but how many. When public schools' budgets continue to contract, parents who care about music, sports, arts, foreign languages, and job skills find themselves trying to fulfill that need through extra-curricular activities. Parents of older kids who'd just like to run track for the fun of it find they're on an all-or-nothing team, with practices every day after school and meets all day Saturday. Multiply that by the number of kids you have, and the next thing you know, every moment of every day is regimented in a military-like schedule, which, by the way, puts you in position of a taxi driver.

It may help to ask your child before signing up for programs how dedicated he'll be to a particular activity. A great number of people feel that "If you're going to do something, you'd better do it right." While it's important to try hard and follow through with what you've registered and paid for, forcing kids into a success-oriented arts or sports program when they just want to wet their whistle may not result in the desired success—far from it. You could get increased defiant behaviors and even increased stress and anxiety. If your child is already displaying defiant behaviors, back off the pressure and consider reducing extracurricular activities to one per child.

Unstructured Time

Now that you've read this, think over your family's schedule: does your child have any unstructured time to play? While idle hands are sometimes a devil's workshop, they're also a creative thinker's workshop. Again, your job as a parent is not to keep your child occupied 100 percent of the time; doing so would impede free thought and development of individuality.

Playing in the Suburbs

Are your kids allowed to play outside? Is it okay for them to set up a basketball hoop, skateboard ramp, or tree house, or does that violate Home Owner's Association (HOA) regulations that keep all the houses looking the same? Do you feel like your kids would be bothering somebody or looked on with suspicion if they made use of the greenbelt areas in your community?

Take the risk. Talk to your HOA if you need to. Kids need free time if they are to come up with any ideas on their own. Problem-solving skills aren't born solely in classrooms and on soccer fields, they're born when a kid wants to make something new—a hand-made kite, a tire swing, a pair of stilts made out of cans and twine, or any other number of practically bygone toys—and has to figure out how by trial and error. *Don't buy these toys so your kid won't have to make them.* Doing so has become common in the last generation or so, and it takes away most of the child's interest in the toy, no matter how ugly it is or how badly it functions. Kids also lose interest in store-bought toys much faster than they do the toys they've made themselves. The same goes for Halloween costumes, Christmas decorations, birthday cards, and so on. What adult hasn't rolled his eyes on Christmas morning because the kids play with the boxes longer than the expensive toys? That says something about the true value of expensive toys. If the toys are more interesting to grown-ups than they are to kids, they're simply not age-appropriate.

 Question

So what should you buy for kids?
There's pressure to have big-ticket items under the Christmas tree and next to the birthday cake. You can buy fewer toys, and if you have to buy something, buy the supplies needed for creative play: boxes, markers, string, glue, wood, nails, paper—whatever is age-appropriate.

Kids need the freedom to do what many people today would consider "wasting time," especially out of doors. A magnifying glass and an anthill *could* result in a fire. They could also result in a biology lesson that is happily learned. They could stimulate interest in related subjects, like how lenses work, why animals colonize, how anthills are made, and so on. They could give a child the opportunity for sustained observation instead of sound bytes delivered through screen time. You wouldn't have to drag a child to the library kicking and screaming to look up these subjects if they were her own idea and her own interest.

Nature Time

For most parents today, spending time in nature is not as easy as it was a generation ago. There are fewer empty lots and back fields, fewer forests and lakes bordering towns, and often, some of what is left has been restricted or deemed off-limits to kids. But nature is important for kids' health: it provides fresh air, exercise, excitement, peace, stability, and those educational buzz concepts like problem-solving skills and cognitive development.

In order for you to help your kids experience the calming and educational benefits of nature, you can do a few things even from your urban apartment or suburban townhome. First, look for the nature you do have access to: learn the names of common flora and fauna in your area, and use the specific names when you point them out to your children. You may have non-native starlings nesting in the local non-native liquid amber trees, but it's something. Show them to your kids, say their names. Naming the plants and animals helps your child distinguish them from each other and notice them more readily.

Second, you can take technology-free nature weekends. You don't need a long, expensive trip to Yellowstone; you can take an overnight stay at a hostel or campground a few hours away. Find a local low-priced facility, book it, and pack dinner, breakfast, sleeping bags, and a few essential supplies. Let your kids figure out what to do when they get there, and if they complain of boredom, it means they need to come more often so they can learn what's not so boring about having the opportunity to think and make their own fun.

 **Essential**

According to Richard Louv, author of *Last Child in the Woods: Saving Our Children from Nature-Deficit Disorder*, nature has become more abstraction than reality for today's kids, resulting in childhoods that are less healthy and frankly, less fun. Ironically, studies have shown nature to be a powerful therapy for ADHD and other issues.

Third, you can make nature microcosms like window gardens and ant farms. They aren't the great outdoors, but they fit in a small living space and give kids the opportunity for learning and peaceful observation. The key here is to refrain from taking over the project. If you're really doing it for your kid, let him have a say in what kinds of herbs to grow, or how many rocks will fit in a terrarium, and resist the urge to maximize the garden's output or micromanage the hummingbird feeder.

Family

Your immediate and extended family can, and hopefully will, be a strong positive influence on your child's growth, development, and moral education. If you are dealing with a defiant child, think carefully about how your family works and simple changes to dynamics that can maximize their positive influences.

Extended Family

You don't have a choice about who your extended family members are. Your parents, siblings, cousins, grandparents, and in-laws are who they are, and you can't change them. Hopefully, they can support you and your efforts to help your child. In order to help them be effective, share what you can with those who need to know first, and do so out of the child's earshot by making a phone call while he's at school or by sending an e-mail. You'll need to let extended family members know if they share caretaking duties or will be coming for an extended visit. For those you see little of and aren't comfortable around, you can keep your child's behavior issues somewhat private.

When it's appropriate, share your observations and strategies with those who need to know. You can ask input from other caregivers, but don't ask permission. When you need to make a mandate, be polite and firm: "Carter is allergic to wheat. Please do not give him wheat or wheat products, like pasta, under any circumstances." Request that people do not roll their eyes or make fun of your parenting practices in front of your kids. If you don't allow your kids to play videogames as much as their cousins, do not allow your brother and his wife to tease or belittle your kids about it. Do allow grandparents—especially those who don't see your child often—to spoil the child within reason and as long as it is safe.

 Alert

If your immediate or extended family has toxic behavior patterns or issues you're not comfortable talking to your child about on your own, ask your local library if they have age-appropriate books that can help. Be aware that some libraries keep books on sexuality, abuse, and other sensitive issues behind the desk, so you may need to ask for them.

Finally, when the family gatherings are over, talk about them with your child. "What did you think of your cousin's new tattoo?" "I thought Aunt Sarah seemed tired and grumpy today, what did you think?" and "Wow, Grandma and Grandpa looked pretty excited about their new video camera!" are good conversation openers for the drive or flight home. Ask for your child's opinion and share your own as well.

When you're not happy about someone else's words or actions, use effective communication skills that focus on behaviors and feelings instead of condemning people. Instead of saying, "Your Uncle Dan is a sleazeball," try, "I'm not comfortable with how Uncle Dan talks about women's bodies. What did you think?" This allows your child to continue loving the family member and to think about the behavior.

Getting Along with Others

As you've learned, kids are strongly influenced by the behaviors of their peers. Don't be afraid of the rest of the world—we all have to live in it. It may seem to you that if you lived in a bucolic city that won "Best City for Raising Kids," or if you had the money to move to a wealthier, more peaceful neighborhood, or if your kid's teacher would stop labeling him, your problems would be solved. But before you pull up your stakes and join a tribe in the Amazon, consider helping your kids gain the social skills they need to succeed in their current environments with their schools, friends, and larger community.

Teaching Empathy

Empathy is the practice of putting yourself in someone else's shoes. Empathy isn't sympathy—it's not feeling sorry for other people—it's similar to following the golden rule with your feelings, and living with the golden rule in your heart.

To teach kids empathy, the simplest thing you can do is ask them to think about others' feelings. "How do you think Jody felt at the playground today when that other girl pushed her?" and "How do you think your brother felt when he came home from school crying?" are fine ways to teach empathy, even when your child is not the aggressor in the situation. Just calling attention to the plight of others is effective.

Next, ask your child to consider how her actions affect others. If your child does or says something hurtful to another child, ask, "How would you feel if he did that to you?" Chances are, this will be met with silence. You can prompt, "Would you like that?" and if there's more silence or a "Yeah!" add, "I don't think you would." Enforce any consequences without making the child feel guilty. If your child shows remorse, say, "It looks like you're feeling sad thinking about how that might have made him feel. Would you like to apologize?" It may take several months of teaching empathy to see results, especially if your child is older.

Anger Management

Diffusing anger is a great skill to teach kids who have an anger problem. You may have heard that anger is not a "real" feeling, and that anger is a way of covering up other feelings of being threatened, vulnerable, sad, or having unmet needs. While it's true that anger stems from these feelings, when someone is angry, you must respect their feelings of anger, not negate them.

Counting to ten is a cliché, but it works. Show your child how to count to ten when she is angry and then respond. Your child may need to blow off some steam by riding a skateboard around the block for a little longer than a count of ten; if so, that's fine.

Once your child has learned to effectively diffuse her anger, you can help her voice the feelings behind it using effective communication skills.

Sharing Your Interests with Your Child

Sharing common interests is another way to have a positive impact on your child's life. Beware that it goes both ways: if you want your child to go fishing with you on Saturday, you'll have a lot more luck if you agree to go to where he wants the following weekend. Taking turns shows you respect your child's interests and genuinely want to be together.

How to Have Fun Together

You can use bonding activities as a starting place to have fun with your child. In addition, you can share some things you like to do. If you like to make jewelry, include a few beads in your son's favorite colors and buy enough findings for him to make one of whatever you're making. If you like sports, invite him to check standings or watch games with you. Don't tell him to forget it if he rolls his eyes. He might join you sometime, and it always feels good to be invited.

Next, offer your child a turn at picking an activity. Your child may want to do something that's completely unpleasant for you, such as going to see a band you can't stand, or play a videogame. Unless the activity is unsafe, and especially if you allow your child to do it without you there, join in once in awhile. Show an interest in it not because you really like it for yourself, but because you're interested in it as an extension of your child and the wonderful person he is. Ask questions like, "What's this for?" "What's the name of this character?" "What does this button do?" and let him take pride in being an expert.

Talking It Over

After an activity is over, talk about it in a nonthreatening way. If it was an activity you picked, explain what you like about it—it makes you feel peaceful, or you enjoy an intellectual challenge, etc. If it was an activity your child picked, observe without judging by remembering interesting things that happened and asking questions about how long your child has been interested in the activity or who else might be involved in it.

Speaking nonjudgmentally about a child's likes and dislikes builds trust between you. Children are much more likely to talk to you about a problem if they don't feel threatened and judged when they've shared their life with you. It doesn't mean you can't have an opinion or enforce consequences when necessary, it just means you're willing to accept them for who they are and take the *behaviors* one step at a time.

CHAPTER 9

Parenting the Defiant Toddler

A ll toddlers defy their parents; it's their nature. However, that doesn't mean that defiance should continue unchecked, or that some defiance in toddlers is cause for concern. This chapter explains how a toddler's mind works when it comes to defiance, and how you can best structure your family's rewards, rules, and consequences to get your strong-willed little one off to the right start.

A Brand-New "Me"

Last year, you had a tiny, helpless baby in your home. This year, you have a strong-willed, energetic adventurer living in your home, and his exciting sensory activity is your thirty-minute cleanup job (while he's off and running to the next wonder). Also, he's just learned the power of the word "no"—by using it himself when you tell him what to do. What's going on?

Inside the Toddler Mind

A toddler's mind is developing at a rapid pace, though not necessarily a steady one. In fits and starts, with lots of spurts, he learns about his surroundings and the emotions of his family and caregivers. For example, he plays with blocks once in awhile for months without being able to stack them successfully, and then one day, wow! He just *gets* it and can stack them on top of each other with ease.

Learning language is one of the primary tasks the toddler's brain undertakes. Little ones need a language-rich environment: one in which a caregiver is almost constantly talking, singing, reading, and gesturing, in order to help them develop fluency. And language itself is another building block, which helps the brain's cells grow and flourish, providing a strong foundation for reasoning, mathematics, music, and more.

A child is also super-sensitive to emotion at this age, picking up on caregiver emotions and internalizing them not just in the moment, but perhaps as part of his permanent personality. Abuse, neglect, and even tension in the home can have adverse affects on a toddler's brain development. Babies and toddlers must be held, touched, talked to, cuddled, and made eye contact with on a regular basis for healthy development of their brains and emotions. In fact, *lack* of this kind of loving interaction can damage the child's social and emotional functioning, leading a child to become unattached and even aggressive. This means there's a definite link between emotional abuse or neglect and defiant behavior.

Why Toddlers Defy Parents

Adventurous little kids want to try everything. What happens when I drop this toy in the toilet? What happens if I scream really, really loud? What happens if I tip this bowl over? What happens if I walk over here to the edge of the sidewalk? What happens if I whack you in the face? What happens if I say "no!"? And what they find out is, "Wow, cool! I have power! I have a direct influence on my surroundings!" including, "Wow! Look how I can make my mom or dad yell, scream, get upset, and carry on!" It starts out as a learning experience and not necessarily as something the child has picked up elsewhere (although that's also quite possible).

Toddlers haven't learned self-control. Having a toddler is similar to having a wild animal in the house—he's hungry, demanding, slightly dangerous, very expensive, and in need of house training. Your toddler doesn't yell "no!" the first time because he's a terrible person or has inherited someone's disagreeable temper; he yells "no!" the first time because he hasn't learned better—yet.

Where this goes next is up to you. He hasn't formed the habit of defiance yet, so you can put safe and reasonable boundaries in place and enforce them, you can ignore the child's behavior, or get furious, and then wonder why it doesn't improve. *Children ask for boundaries.* If you allow a "no!" or a whack in the face to slip by, expect to see it again soon. You've just taught your toddler —a walking information sponge, a super-computing learning machine—that defiance gets results, and you've also sent a mixed message that he needs to follow up on to find out, once and for all, if that behavior is allowed. He's defied you and wants to know: what are you going to do about it? Do you care about him enough to back up what you say?

Independence or Defiance?

Toddlers are also fighting for their independence. They strive for autonomy at the same time they strive to prove themselves valuable members of their family, so they often insist on "me do it."

Allow your toddler to slowly build the skills necessary for being both an autonomous individual and a valuable, contributing member of the household. The desire to practice new skills should not be confused with defiance. Building these skills is not neat or quick, so young children should be allowed to:

- Make a mess outdoors with dirt, water, sticks, rocks, and so on
- Make a mess with paint and other hands-on art activities
- Explore safe cooking activities that are sensory-rich, such as stirring dough
- "Help" with household chores such as laundry, toy pickup, sweeping, and wiping up spills

- Practice self-care skills such as brushing teeth, combing hair, getting dressed, and using the toilet when ready, with an adult at arm's reach to help and check for thoroughness

In addition, children should be involved in the cleanup after these activities and instructed all the while in the rules surrounding the activities.

 Alert

> There will be times when you can't allow your child to help with household chores because it's not safe. Or, if you have a child who is easily frustrated, and you can see he's usually exhausted at night, you might need to "save him from himself" and insist on brushing his teeth for him for a few more months.

If you allow your child plenty of time to practice building skills so he doesn't feel squashed or oppressed, he will be more receptive to you when you need to postpone new skills for safety reasons.

What You May Be Experiencing

As with weather, the only constant with toddlers is change. Every morning when they wake up, they're much more than they were the night before. Perhaps that's why they so desperately need stability from the adults in their lives—they need to know they can depend on their environment for stability if they can't depend on themselves.

Taking Normal Defiance Seriously

Defiance is normal in toddlers. That does *not* mean you should tolerate it; in fact, in order for behaviors to continue on a normal path, you must reward good behavior, set up rules, and enforce consequences when those rules are broken. A child who says "no!" or tries to get away with breaking rules is behaving normally. But don't kick back and ignore what's going on; rise to your child's challenge and enforce consequences consistently so she can build the kinds of habits that will make your life *much* easier in the coming months and years.

Regressions and Frustration

Because children are developing in fits and starts and assimilating so much information, they have frequent regressions. Potty training is the most famous area of regressions, partly because parents want it so badly that they are ultra-aware of their child's progress. All children will experience regressions, and they should not be punished, shamed, or embarrassed for them. Instead, expect the regressions, and wait until your child is completely ready before creating rules around using new skills like potty training. Consistency and encouragement will help your child solidify new habits.

Don't be surprised if an anxious child is also easily frustrated. Children who are anxious about perfection set high expectations for themselves from an early age, and become extremely frustrated when they can't meet them. If you think your child is becoming a perfectionist, set a "counter-example" by pointing out your own mistakes: "Oops, I forgot to buy mayonnaise at the store!" Then show that it's okay: "Darn. Oh, well, it's okay to forget something. I can always get mayonnaise next time. No big deal."

Toddlers, Change, and Stress

Toddlers are super sensitive to change. Helping a toddler make what may seem like a simple transition, even one the toddler wants—going from a crib to a bed, or having a new baby in the home, for example—can require the kind of strategy, support, and planning normally reserved for launching a new product at a major corporation.

To the extent possible, keep a toddler's life routine. You will probably feel very bored by this. That's okay. Especially if you're a stay-at-home parent, build some time with other people into your routine so you don't feel isolated or stifled—an exercise class with other parents, or a weekly meal with neighbors or extended family are helpful ways to make contact with others and add variety to your life.

 Question

How do we prepare for a new baby?
A new sibling is an earth-shattering change for a toddler. Once your pregnancy is on track, begin preparing your toddler by talking frequently about the new baby and reading lots of books together about what it will be like to have a new baby in the home.

When change is unavoidable, be advised that it will cause significant stress for your child. Regressions in behaviors you thought were mastered are normal, as is anxiety and clinginess. A little extra bonding time will probably help relieve some of your child's stress and improve behavior.

Signs That Something Is Wrong

Defiance is normal. What isn't? While ODD is extremely rare and virtually impossible to diagnose in toddlers, some behaviors could point to other problems that need medical or psychiatric attention.

ODD, Autism, and Developmental Disorders

Because part of the criteria for diagnosing ODD is a pattern of defiant behaviors persisting at least six months, it's hard to diagnose a toddler as having ODD—he just doesn't have enough history! The same goes for ADHD. However, you're the parent, and you know your child better than anyone else, so if you think the child's behaviors are on track to ODD or ADHD, contact a child psychologist to talk about decreasing the risk now. In addition, consider that your child's behaviors could be symptoms of another disorder, as described below.

Children who appear uninterested in social interaction and who are extremely inflexible regarding changes to their routine may be autistic. Unlike ODD, autism usually includes significant language impairment. Autistic children may be able to use speech, but they may not do so normally or for the purposes of communicating with others so much as to get basic needs met or as part of a preoccupation with a particular activity.

There are other developmental disorders that are less common than autism but may have some symptoms in common with ODD. Autism is part of a broader classification called "pervasive developmental disorder" (PDD); there is also a type of autism called Asperger syndrome in which language develops more normally than in typical autism. If you believe your child's behaviors could be symptomatic of one of these disorders, or if you suspect your child may show signs of mental retardation, visit a pediatric specialist as soon as possible for early diagnosis and the best possible treatment plan.

Illness, Injury, and Trauma

If you suspect your child has had an illness, injury, or other trauma that has affected brain development and therefore behavior, you should visit a pediatric specialist as soon as possible. Especially if your child is adopted, or has been cared for by others for a significant amount of time, you may not have complete and accurate information on the history of her care, and a toddler with even normal language development may not be able to tell you if there has been an injury or trauma. Any concerns you have about your child's brain development should be addressed immediately.

How to Bond and Create a Safe Environment

Because toddlers are so sensitive to change and are in the crucial period for forming bonds with caregivers, some special considerations for bonding and creating a secure environment are in order.

Caregivers and Love

If you're like most families today, you need two sources of income to make ends meet. If neither parent can stay home with the child, you're probably one of millions of parents whose toddler is in some type of extended care, whether in your own home, in a neighborhood day care, in an educational daycare/preschool environment, or at a relative's home. Remember that children form an attachment to one primary caregiver, with all other bonds being subsequent. If you want yourself or your spouse to be the primary attachment figure in your child's life, you must take steps to bond during your free time.

 Essential

Time alone with Mom or Dad is a very attractive reward to children of this age, especially if a new sibling has entered the picture. Carving out half-hour blocks for simple playing or reading books together can go a long way toward improving toddler behavior.

There are a few things you can do to strengthen your bond with your toddler. Spend time cuddling, reading, playing, and talking. If you want to build a bond with your child and have little time to do so, avoid watching television together or going on "big" outings to amusement parks or other high-stimulus environments where you'll spend more time interacting with the environment than with each other. If you do have the disposable income for this type of activity, consider spending it instead on help around the home so you can spend more one-on-one time with the toddler.

Routine and Security

You can't protect your child from the outside world completely or forever. However, when your child is a toddler, it's worth a try. Routine and security help toddlers have the calm and peace they need to master their new skills and develop healthy emotions, so put your best effort into insulating your child from stress and change by establishing a daily rhythm that is somewhat predictable. At the least, try to have a nightly "wind-down" routine that moves from dinner to bed in a series of steps that are repeated and end with the child in bed at the same time every night. (This will also help everyone get a better night's sleep.) Don't throw bedtime out the window more than a few times a year. Maintaining this routine will help the child feel stable when stressors *do* occur, such as a move, marital tension, or a new baby.

How to Have a Dialogue with Your Toddler

"Dialogue" and "toddler" may seem to some people like two words that don't belong in the same sentence, but a closer look at children's development of language and your role in it proves otherwise. Little children are watching and listening to what's going on around them, and you can provide enriching input, harmful input, or no input at all, which can be just as devastating.

The Building Blocks of Language

When you teach your child how to wash his hands, you're teaching him more than just hygiene. You're also teaching social etiquette, giving him a chance to practice coordination, giving him a sense of pride in himself, and, though you may not realize it, teaching him language at the same time. Talking to your child, who can't talk back the way an adult can, isn't as one-sided as it seems; you're talking to someone who is soaking up not just the content of what you're saying, but the system by which you're saying it. When you say, "Soapy! Are you all soapy?" you're teaching your child vocabulary, inflection, pronunciation, and how to form a question.

Without this kind of interaction, children can't learn language. They need *lots* of input to develop fluency. What better conversation topic than loving words to strengthen bonds, communicate your values, and sow the seeds of empathy?

Communicating Your Values to Your Toddler

A toddler's worldview is self-centered, and "me, me, me" is his refrain. That's normal, but allowing him to remain so isn't: now's the time to start sowing the seeds of empathy. The first step is to give names to feelings. When reading a book, show him the characters' expressions and name them: "Look, the monkey is sad." or "Yay! The little boy is excited now!" are ways to narrate feelings portrayed in illustrations and photos. Also, help your child name his own feelings: "Oh, the crayon broke. It looks like you're disappointed. Are you disappointed?" Develop a vocabulary of feeling words.

 Alert

> Be sure to make a distinction between being responsible for one's actions and being responsible for others' feelings, or your child will be vulnerable to guilt-trips. So, if your child breaks someone's toy, instead of saying, "You made him feel sad; go say sorry," say, "He's crying now. How do you think he feels? What can you do?"

Next, implement the Golden Rule. Whenever your child hurts another person—because even the most well-behaved children do hurt others at some point—say, "How would you like it if somebody did that to you? Would you like it?" Then, elicit a feeling word:

"How would you feel? Do you think you might feel scared, or embarrassed?" If your child appears remorseful, say, "It looks like you feel sorry. Would you like to go apologize? I'll come with you." Support your child during an embarrassing apology, but don't apologize for him. He must do it himself to successfully make amends.

Finally, keep praise for apologies at a minimum, or your toddler will make a "First I hit, then I apologize, then everybody gives me attention" connection that could result in further aggressive behavior.

Easy on the Logic

Toddlers are capable of simple logic: I kick the ball, it moves forward; I throw food, I get put in time out. They are not capable of more than a few steps in a logical sequence: going to sleep too late tonight makes me grumpy tomorrow and that's why I end up in trouble and can't have dessert tomorrow night and spend an hour throwing a fit, causing me to stay up too late yet again. When there's more than one or two steps of logic involved, the kind thing to do is to take control and say, "This is the rule, therefore we are doing it," and end it there.

In addition, toddlers think in terms of the concrete (here and now) rather than the abstract (ideas, the past, and the future). "Don't open Mommy's purse," is more effective than, "I really don't want you playing in my purse because my checkbook is in there and if it gets torn that's like tearing money, which . . . ." Lengthy explanations tend to be ineffective; a toddler who appears to be paying rapt attention is more likely enjoying the delay of consequences and the pleasure of watching his effect on you. When you say no to a toddler, don't discuss it. No is no.

Sample Reward-Rule-Consequence Scenarios

Now you have the tools to put into action for toddlers. The structure in a toddler's environment should be very positive and focused primarily on rewards, the "peanuts" that lead your child step by step in the desired direction.

How to Reward Good Behavior

There's a skeleton you can use for potty training, going to school, eating vegetables, and so on. Start with just one behavior, whichever is most important to you. (This doesn't mean all other rules are off, but put your focus on one you think will be difficult but doable for your toddler and is very important to you.) When your child is developmentally ready to begin working on the new skill, introduce it ahead of time in a gentle but firm way that makes the activity seem positive and fun: "Do you see that building? That's where you're going to take swimming lessons! Wow! Look at all the kids getting ready!" or "This is your potty. It's just for you! See how it's just your size?" Let the idea sink in, and come back to it once or twice. Build some excitement.

 Question

What if I need to elicit a good behavior that's totally unpleasant, like behaving during a medical procedure?
If it's a one-time procedure, don't build it into your rewards program. If your child must have the procedure repeatedly, you can use a rewards program, but don't deceive your child by saying it's going to be fun.

Then, cut a large sheet of paper or buy a piece of poster board and put the child's name on it. Take your child with you to a store with a nice selection of stickers, and ask her to pick out a sheet of reasonably priced stickers (you might select a few for her to pick from to narrow it down). Then say, "Every time you (whatever the skill is), you get to put one sticker on your rewards chart." Let the child put the stickers up herself. Cheer her on.

When the skill is mastered and your child is "over" the reward chart, finalize the program by congratulating her again and taking a photo of her standing in front of the sticker-filled reward chart before you take it down. Place the photo on the refrigerator for a while.

How to Decrease Problem Behavior

First, try to reframe the behavior—instead of a rule *against* staying up too late, can you make a rule *for* going to bed on time? Those are actions you can reward, and rewards are much more effective than punishing problem behavior.

However, there are some behaviors, like hitting, that you can't ignore or reframe. Choose one or two definite no-no's that are a current problem, such as hitting or running into the street, and make a rule against them. Be prepared—your child will test you, so don't make a rule you can't enforce.

Announce the new rule just before there is an opportunity for the problem behavior. For example, announce a rule against hitting just before your child goes to play at someone's house. Say, "There is no hitting. Keep your hands to yourself." Plan to be extremely vigilant on this day and on the next few days your child will have an opportunity to break the rule. When your child breaks the rule, react immediately by restating the rule, "No hitting," and placing your child in time out for one to two minutes per year of the child's age. Do not react to screaming and tantrum-throwing. Do not engage in a dialogue or reason with your child. When the time is up and your child has been quiet for a moment or two, say, "Time out is over. You can get up now," and repeat the rule, "No hitting."

CHAPTER 10

Parenting the Defiant Three-to-Five-Year-Old

Parents of three-to-five-year-olds often comment that their child is now more of a person. By this, they don't mean babies and toddlers aren't human; they mean preschool-aged children have greater powers of reasoning and can interact and talk with adults in a more equal way. These new capabilities bring about a whole new spectrum of ways your child can defy you—and ways you can help her be a happy, anxiety-free, cooperative little person.

The "Real Little Person"

What's going on with a preschool-aged child? Are his fears genuine, or is he just pushing your buttons for the fun of it? Perhaps your spouse or another loving adult has pulled you aside and indicated—lovingly or otherwise—that your child is running the show and you're being manipulated. Is that true?

Inside the Preschooler Mind

Without a trace, your toddler has vanished. In his place is a preschooler who can empathize with others, show remorse, and have a fully fluent conversation that includes abstract elements. Yet he's still very much a little kid, dependent on adults for help with some or even lots of self-care, reassurance, and instruction in preschool skills, social skills, language, and other enrichment.

Between three and five years of age, children are learning to recognize and scratch out letters, use scissors, paint representative pictures, and use more specialized vocabulary, all important skills for school preparedness. So is the ability to master the native language (though mistakes are frequently made), using it to understand stories, interact with others, express needs (including emotional needs), and learn to be a part of a culture. Finally, social skills, including taking turns, sharing, respecting others' feelings, and respecting authority are important tools to learn during this age. As a parent, you must help your child develop these skills, and defiant children need extra help and strategy to develop social skills appropriately.

Why Three-to-Five-Year-Olds Defy Parents

There are two reasons kids in this age group defy their parents. The first is to mask fears, avoid unpleasant tasks, or gain some sense of control in a chaotic, adult-controlled world. If your child routinely refuses to comply with a specific task—putting his shoes on, for example—troubleshoot the problem and also ask your child why this is such a problem. Could it be because he can't find them, because they hurt his feet, because they are difficult to put on, or because he doesn't want to get ready to go to school? If so, explore some possible solutions: always putting the shoes in the same place when entering the house, checking to see that they fit correctly, buying shoes that fasten with Velcro, or addressing separation anxiety. Once you have found a reasonable solution, stick with it; you can continue to monitor it, but don't let your child know, because this could lead to the other reason kids defy their parents.

The second reason kids of this age set defy their parents is to get a reaction from them. This is obnoxious, defiant behavior that is done on purpose and ends with everybody angry and the whole family suffering. These behaviors include yelling and screaming indoors and just generally making home life unpleasant for everyone. When you ask the child to stop, the child refuses to comply, and you're left with a vicious cycle of defiant behavior and ineffective discipline.

 Question

Is my kid manipulating me?
If a loved one or a teacher has indicated you might be getting manipulated by your child, respect how difficult it probably was for the loved one to bring it to your attention, and consider the possibility. If, however, a stranger points it out, check with someone who knows you for a second opinion.

What You May Be Experiencing

To be more specific, defiant behaviors aren't just yelling and screaming, they include passive defiance, nasty physical and verbal explosions, and lying and deceitfulness. By this age, children are capable of a small amount of scheming and plotting, and are aware that their behavior affects others; and they are perfectly capable of adhering to your rules.

The Passive Defiant

Procrastinating and pretending to be lost in thought (which can become so ingrained, the child actually becomes lost in thought) are two big acts of passive defiance. They're "sins of omission," so to speak: you ask your child to brush her teeth, and twenty minutes later, she's still standing in front of the mirror with her toothbrush, though she's been capable of brushing her teeth for years. Often, she's even very sweet and apologetic about "forgetting," or wants to tell you how she's caught up in a sophisticated fantasyland that amazes you for how creative it is. *This is still defiance.* If you have told your child to do something and it's not getting done although she is fully capable of doing it, she is defying you, and you must take action or it will get worse.

Explosions

On the other hand, back talk, tantrums, and hitting are examples of "explosions," and in that order escalate from least disruptive to most disruptive. Back talk is common and normal; tantrums are common and normal but should be decreasing to virtually nil during these years; hitting is unacceptable and is not normal if it happens regularly. Again, the normalcy of defiant behaviors doesn't mean that any of them should be excused or tolerated; it means that your concern as a parent should be immediate and direct rather than long-term. It means you should take swift action so that your child's behavior *continues* to develop normally.

Lying and Deceitfulness

By the time a child is four years old, she's capable of the abstract thought necessary to lie, hide, or sneak something in order to extend fun or delay boring or unpleasant activities. In order to be an effective parent now and in the future, you need to foster an environment of honesty and trust starting now, so you can't tolerate lying or deceitfulness, ever.

 Essential

A positive first step toward an honest environment is to read with your child a kids' book about telling the truth. This will provide a framework for future discussions on honesty, and help cement the idea over time as you incorporate the book into your child's collection.

The best way to prevent lying or deceitfulness is by helping your child stay out of trouble. When you think your child is on the cusp of a lie, step in and say, "It looks like you're feeling embarrassed/ashamed. Did you break the window/flush the toy down the toilet?" Give your child the chance to tell the truth, and reward her with hugs and encouragement when she does. Say something such as,

"I know it was hard for you to tell the truth because you didn't want to get in trouble. Thank you for doing that." If a rule has been broken, you must follow through with consequences, but you can do it with an understanding smile, and can reward the child for telling the truth once the consequences have been completed. A public recognition of the child's courage, such as telling your spouse about how brave your child was to tell the truth, is helpful. Note: this love, attention, and reward becomes invalid if your child confesses *after* you've handed down a consequence.

Signs That Something Is Wrong

At this age, many children are entering preschool or a daycare environment, and for the first time, they'll have other adults who are more than just caretakers, but educators: people who are experienced at helping kids learn, and who might have an idea if there is a problem that interferes with a child's academic or social development.

ODD, ADHD, and Other Disorders

Children in the three-to-five-year set can be diagnosed with ODD and ADHD, since they now have enough history of behaviors to be eligible for meeting the criteria for diagnoses. In addition, children this age can be depressed or have an anxiety disorder. Finally, theories of a new disorder, known primarily as sensory integration dysfunction, postulate that some young children are hyper-sensitive to stimuli, with tactile stimuli being a big attention-grabber for parents who are frustrated by children who can't stand sock seams, clothing seams, and tags in their shirts. Sensory integration dysfunction is not yet recognized by the APA, and these symptoms can be linked to other neurological conditions. Again, if you feel your child has symptoms of these or another disorder, contact a pediatrician, and try to minimize other stressors in your child's life in the meantime.

Illness, Injury, and Trauma

During the preschool years, children learn to ride trikes and/or bikes, jump on the couch and bed, climb trees, swim, and many other wonderful yet potentially dangerous activities. As a preventative measure, talk to your child about safety precautions and why we use them, and when you see your child about to do something dangerous that's not an immediate emergency, like perching on the back of the couch, ask, "Do you think that's safe?" Your child is now old enough to judge some behaviors and make cause-effect connections; so help him practice these skills by giving him a chance to reevaluate dangerous behavior.

If you child sustains an injury that could affect development, visit the nearest emergency room. Nonemergent illness or trauma that can affect development should also be evaluated by a pediatric specialist at the first possible opportunity.

Daycare and Preschool Issues

You may find that your child's behavior at and attitude toward school or daycare fluctuates some over these years. At first, the child may be apprehensive, then grow used to the routine, then refuse to go for a few months, and finally grow content with the arrangement again. Here's how to handle problem behavior surrounding going to preschool or daycare.

Problem Behavior at School

If your child's teacher has expressed concerns about her behavior at school, you must do two things: uphold and enforce rules, and evaluate what has been happening to determine if there are any other factors that could be contributing to the defiant or problematic behavior.

First, it's extremely important that you uphold the school's authority, rules, and consequences. If you don't, you're setting yourself up for *many* more parent-teacher conferences in the coming years. You must teach your child to respect the school rules and the rights of others by letting the school's consequences stand. Do you privately think that the teacher is an idiot, the other kids are brats, and the rules are for people who can't think for themselves? If so, you're passing this entitled mindset to your child and it will work to her disadvantage in the long run. Other people don't enjoy being around someone with a chip on her shoulder; a team player is the more successful individual.

 Alert

> You may have thought separation anxiety was just for toddlers. Pre-school children can experience a phase of separation anxiety, too. If this describes what you're going through, increase the one-on-one time to strengthen your bond. Cuddling and reading in the morning before school can be especially effective.

Next, consider if there are any other circumstances at the school or in your child's life that could be contributing to problem behavior, which your child can't or won't articulate. Is she the only five-year-old in a classroom of threes? Is she getting enough sleep? Does she think you or the school are asking for academic perfection? If so, troubleshoot possible ways to remedy the situation *without* undermining the school's authority, and solicit the teacher's input for possible solutions.

Angel at School, Defiant at Home

There are many aggressive people—adults and children alike—who are the picture of stability at school or work, but who terrorize their families at home. Ironically, people show their worst sides to those they love most! This could be because they feel "safe" at home and let down their guard.

You need to be concerned about the possibility that your child could be exhibiting problem behavior at home in reaction to frustration or anxiety at school or daycare. If so, troubleshoot what could be going on at school or daycare, talk with your child about that environment and what goes on there, and if you need to remove your child from the facility, re-read the end of Chapter 2, on weaning from unsafe bonds.

How to Bond and Create a Secure Environment

Your child is not a toddler anymore, and as the parent, you've grown, too: you're more than just a person who fulfills a baby's physical and emotional needs, you're now in a position to facilitate your child's intellectual growth and self-esteem. You also have a chance to be a real superhero to your child.

Caregivers and Love

If your child is in daycare or preschool, be extra sure to spend one-on-one time with him. For a preschool-aged child, time goes by much more slowly, and waiting until the weekend to "catch up" with Mom or Dad is like waiting an eternity. So much happens in a child's development during this time that bonding only two days a week can be detrimental to emotional development. You'll need to make sure your child gets daily one-on-one time with at least one parent, even if it's only for a few minutes.

You may find that even though the morning rush is hectic, building in a few more minutes for reading a morning story or having a five-minute pre-daycare cuddle can improve behavior much more than waiting until evening. Little kids are "morning people"; make sure they get some of you during their best waking hours instead of only at night when they're cranky.

Providing Enrichment

If your child stays at home with you, or is in a daycare environment with little structure, you'll need to provide enrichment to build school readiness skills. You don't need to memorize the state capitals or devise any other intense, goal-oriented lessons; on the contrary, the pressure to perform can be too much for young children. Instead, provide plenty of opportunity to paint, use scissors, play outdoors, sing songs, learn about the natural world, read books, count, and begin recognizing letters and numbers. Check your local school district's requirements for kindergarten readiness, and see that your child can do the basics, such as writing her name. For extra fun, check your local paper or monthly family magazine for free and low-cost activities such as puppet shows, nature walks, and library story times.

Be a Superhero: Eliminate Bad Guys

Preschool-aged children may not be ready for many of the cartoons, movies, and other media that is supposedly devised just for them. Most shows with a plot have a bad guy to help drive the action, but little kids don't need bad guys. Bad guys increase anxiety, and can even lead to nightmares; violence can increase defiant behavior. You will be a superhero in your kid's life if you eradicate movies with bad guys and give your child a calmer, safer perspective in life.

 **Question**

Whose movie is this?
If you find you enjoy yourself while watching kids' movies, step back and consider if your kid is getting the same jokes, or is just caught up in the pace. Movies are made to appeal to parents as much as kids, because parents buy the tickets and the ensuing merchandise. The films may not be age-appropriate.

A loose plot or none at all is all that's necessary for a young child. Nature videos, music performances, and kids' sing-a-long variety or educational shows can be just as entertaining, and are much less likely to induce nightmares. If you are bored with this type of programming, remember that it's not intended for adults and shouldn't appeal to you as much as it does to your child.

How to Have a Dialogue with Your Three-to-Five-Year-Old

Your child is now old enough to have a real conversation: listening, thinking, evaluating, judging, and responding with ideas of her own. Now's the time for real conversations!

Communicating Your Values

As you did with safety issues, you can use your child's own conscience to shape her behavior now. You can ask, "Do you think your friends will like it if you bring a toy but don't want to share it?" "Do you think your brother might want us to pick up a sandwich for him, too?" and "What do you think might happen if you leave your bike lying in the street?" Similarly, instead of re-creating the rules of the world, you can take the pressure off yourself by reading aloud the signs posted in public places that are relevant to your child. You can say, "Let's read the rules on the shopping cart seat. See the picture with a line through it? That means no standing up in the cart. Why do you think there's a rule against that?" By using these questions as open-ended paths to conscience, you can communicate your values to your child without preaching.

Expecting Good Manners

Talking about good manners can seem old-fashioned and stuffy to some people. If it does to you, it might help to rephrase these beliefs in twenty-first century dogma: "being nice builds social capital," "connections get the job done," and "everybody likes a team player." No matter how you slice it, good manners never go out of style.

In order for your child to use good manners (saying "please" and "thank you," greeting others, sharing, and waiting her turn), you must model them in your interactions with others and in your interactions with her. In other words, if you want your child to say, "Can you please pass the butter?" to you, you must say so to her instead of reaching past her like she doesn't exist. In front of others, gentle reminders like "What do you say?" are helpful. Don't stand in for your child; insist that *she* say thank you when someone has done her a favor or given her a gift.

Sample Reward-Rule-Consequence Scenarios

Now you have the tools to put into action for three-to-five-year-olds. The structure in a preschooler's environment should still be very positive and focused primarily on rewards. In addition, you can now start to develop your child's conscience.

How to Reward Good Behavior

With children of this age group, you still need to use immediate rewards, however, you can start to use immediate rewards that build and can be "cashed in" for bigger—but not too big—tangible rewards. Take this one in baby steps: children of this age group can learn to delay gratification for a little while, but not forever, and big rewards aren't as effective as small and medium-sized ones.

Again, start with one or two specific positive behaviors you'd like to see more of, like saying "please" and "thank you," picking up toys, or going to bed without a fuss. Set up one of two rewards programs:

- For behaviors you'd like to see throughout the day, a sticker program like the one for toddlers, but which has a better prize for every five stickers is effective. Five stickers can equal a "date" with Mom or Dad, an extra story at night, or choosing the dinner menu.

- For behaviors you'd like to see more of once a day, such as picking up toys or eating vegetables, use the daily fun activities to your advantage: you can watch TV after you've picked up your toys; you can have dessert after you've eaten your vegetables. It's key that the rewards are given the same day, preferably immediately, in order to be effective.

Explain the rewards to your child, and that they are effective immediately. In addition, remember that your praise, hugs, and attention are huge motivators for your child, so pile them on when you see the behaviors you want, and you'll get more of them!

How to Decrease Problem Behaviors

On the other hand, there are other behaviors you'll need to decrease, and time out is still most effective, so you can follow the consequences outlined in the previous chapter. As a reminder, be sure to let all of your child's earned rewards stand. Once a reward has been earned or a sticker placed on the chart, do not take it away, or your child could become very upset and increase defiant behavior. Finally, remember to make only rules you can enforce, and then enforce them vigilantly.

CHAPTER 11

Parenting the Defiant Five-to-Ten-Year-Old

Some parents call the five-to-ten years the "golden years" of parenting: the time when the child is "self-contained." Your child is able to dress and feed herself, sleep through the night, use the bathroom, and have a rational conversation, before the intensity and turbulence of the teen years. For some parents, this time is the eye in the hurricane, but if you're dealing with a defiant child, you may experience little relief. Take heart and take action; you can still influence deep change in your child's behavioral and thinking patterns at this age.

Five-to-Ten-Year-Olds and Defiance

During these years, your child is maturing physically, socially, emotionally, and academically, but in much more subtle steps than before. Growth is slower and steadier, which usually makes for a calmer kid, but defiance still happens.

Inside the Five-to-Ten-Year-Old Mind

At this age, you may see your child struggle in some areas (academic or otherwise) and flourish in others while you alternatively anguish and swell with pride. It's important to celebrate and build on your child's successes, refrain from comparing him to others who do better, and gently but firmly support your child in areas where he's having trouble. Again, these areas aren't always academic, they can be social, athletic, spiritual, logical, and so on. These are the years when your child's aptitudes and desires will develop into the strengths that later lead him to higher learning and career choices.

 Essential

Multiple intelligences (MI) theory was developed by psychologist Howard Gardner in the early 1980s. It originally encompassed seven types of intelligences, though more have been added, and has been instrumental in broadening schools' curricula to consider other learning styles. However, it has been widely criticized as being Gardner's opinion and impossible to prove.

Even if you subscribe to the idea that your child's particular strengths are not given much consideration in a traditional school setting, you can't very well excuse him from classroom learning. For one thing, your analysis could be wrong. For another, you not only undermine his education, you give him the mistaken impression that if a system doesn't work for him, he can drop out of it and still be fine, which will severely impact his ability to get along with others and hold a job as an adult. What's more, it's extremely rare that a child is so smart he gets bad grades out of boredom; much more likely is that he hasn't learned yet how to harness his potential in the classroom. Only requiring that he actually do the work will help him, and the last section of this chapter will show you how to do that.

Why Five-to-Ten-Year-Olds Defy Authority

Even at this age, it still comes down to rewards, rules, and consequences, and the need for consistency. Though you need to adapt the rules for an older child, they are still rules, and everybody in the house must respect them, with exceptions happening only a few times per year. Without plenty of rewards and praise for good behavior and rules and consequences that are consistently enforced, your child will continue to defy you.

Children also defy authority when they find a new weapon to use: the power of reason. "It's time for bed," can be met with, "But I have a science project I have to finish!" "But I haven't had dinner!" and "But you said I could watch a movie tonight!" In these cases, repeating the rule is warranted, but it must be kept short so that the child doesn't begin using conversation as a way of procrastinating. You'll have to strike an assertive balance between the passive, "Okay, I guess you can stay up fifteen more minutes," (or quietly allowing the child to disobey) and the tyrannical yet still ineffective, "Get your butt in bed or I'll spank you so hard . . . !" responses. An effective response to any of the above is, "That's true, and it's also true that you've had plenty of time to do other things. Now it's time for bed." If your child doesn't comply within five seconds, issue the consequences. As for the excuse of a science project that needs finishing, your child will also have consequences at school, and you can't save him from them, or he will repeat the same behavior next time.

What You May Be Experiencing

School is your child's second home now, a place where she spends more waking hours than she does at home. Any behavior problems that aren't pointed out to you by a teacher are almost certainly noticed by her, and the teacher can be an ally for you—and your child—if you treat her with respect and attention to the classroom as a whole.

Problems at School

If your child's teacher has indicated your child has a behavior problem, take it seriously. If you haven't had one yet, ask for a private conference and gather as much information as you can. This can be scary for you; you may be surprised to find it can be scary for the teacher, too. If you would like your child's teacher to help you and your child, forge a respectful relationship by empathizing with his difficult task—teaching a large number of children within a strict curriculum guideline while budget cuts make each day more difficult than the last—and listening calmly. Don't be defensive or rationalize your child's behavior. No matter what the teacher says or how wrong you think he is, thank him for taking the time to speak to you, and ask if he has any specific suggestions for remedying the problem at hand. Next, take the information home, discuss it with your partner, and either implement the solution or ask the teacher and administration for more information, resources, or feedback.

Learning disabilities are another problem at school, for two reasons. First, if the problem hasn't been diagnosed, your child could be struggling for no apparent reason and growing extremely frustrated and angry while watching other children "get" lessons with ease; in fact, mistaking a learning disability for defiance could infuriate the child even more. If you suspect this is the case, talk with the teacher and ask for academic testing. Second, if the problem *has* been diagnosed, the child could be embarrassed about special, yet helpful treatment, and could be longing to be "normal." If you suspect this is the case, you might help your child by explaining that nobody is "normal," and that each person has a separate journey in life, always with "bumps" in the road. Watching movies and reading true-life accounts of people who have overcome disability can help.

Extracurricular Activities

Many children this age are involved in one or several extracurricular activities, from Girl Scouts to karate or soccer, to piano or language lessons. Since schools have so little money for extracurricular programs, most parents have to schedule and pay for them outside of the school day, so evenings and weekends are full of games, recitals, practices, and programs that either continue steadily or change up with every holiday, vacation, and change in seasons. While this sounds crazy, and it definitely can be, parents and kids sign up for it because it's valuable education, and it's socially important.

If your child is having a behavior problem during an extracurricular activity, listen empathetically with the instructor or coach, and observe a class or lesson. Instructors and coaches may not have as much training as a schoolteacher, but they probably still have a good reason for reaching out to you. If you can't remedy the behavior simply, you can end the extracurricular activity. Your child may not like it, and you may have to consider other childcare options, but your child may actually benefit more from the downtime—if it is replaced with activities other than screen time—than she may from the extracurricular activity.

Signs That Something Is Wrong

Now that your child spends less time with you, it might be harder to spot the symptoms that something is wrong. If you need more information, remember that you can observe your child at school for a day. If you decide to do so, check with administration first, and if you decide to tell your child of your plans, just say that you want to see what school is like rather than tell him you want to see if something is wrong.

Learning Disabilities

If your child has a learning disability (LD), his teacher may be the first to point out something's wrong, but you might have to wait for that to happen. In a packed classroom, a learning disability can go unnoticed, especially if the child has pride or perfectionist traits that keep him from expressing what's wrong. Meanwhile, he'll grow more frustrated and angry each day. Children with LD also tend to struggle socially, missing body language cues and other complex, subtle patterns in their peers' behavior. If your child is doing poorly in school and you suspect LD, ask the teacher for a conference to talk about your concerns. You can also request academic testing. See Chapter 17 for more information.

 Alert

> The "homicidal triad" refers to three behaviors that are linked with homicidal behavior later in life. If your five-to-ten-year-old or older child displays chronic bed-wetting, fire-starting, and cruelty toward animals, it is extremely important that you seek outside help from a child psychiatrist immediately.

Illness, Injury, and Trauma

Though your child is more capable of explaining the details of playground accidents and headaches at this age, you are less likely to witness them firsthand. Take any account of a head injury or chronic headaches seriously. Note that headaches can be psychosomatic (symptoms of being emotionally upset) and should be first checked by a pediatrician; then seek out a mental health professional for help treating underlying issues of anxiety, fear, trauma, or depression.

Five-to-Ten-Year-Olds and ODD

If a child has ODD but wasn't diagnosed in the preschool years, chances are the symptoms will become unmistakable now and could even develop into the more severe CD. It's at this age, too, that a diagnosis of ADHD is made because the symptoms become more apparent and disruptive to classroom learning.

ODD and ADHD

Remember from Chapter 4 that kids with ODD can get worse without *professional* intervention. This does not mean you're a failure or can't parent effectively. It does mean that your whole family can benefit from the support, structure, and perspective that therapy can offer, and that your child's behavior is severe enough that new parenting strategies must be undertaken quickly and with extra help. If you know or suspect your child has ODD, seek professional help.

Also remember that ODD and ADHD often go hand in hand: about half of kids with ADHD also have ODD. If your child already has ADHD, or if you suspect he does, consider the possibility that he could also have ODD. This doesn't mean you should go through life thinking your cup is half empty; only by confronting obstacles can you overcome them.

Warning Signs of CD

As explained in Chapter 4, ODD can develop into the more severe CD if it is left untreated. At this age, a child with ODD has enough history that a CD diagnosis is possible, so if you see your child's behavior worsening to the point where he bullies, steals, physically harms people and animals, carries a weapon, damages property, or breaks into homes, cars, or buildings, seek immediate help.

How to Teach Skills That Win Friends and Admiration

As you've seen in the chapters on rewards, rules, and consequences, stopping bad behavior isn't enough to help a child grow into a well-rounded, satisfied, happy adult. You must also nurture skills that benefit the child, and a key way to benefit your child is to help her win friends and admiration.

How to Have Friends

If you want to have friends, you have to be a friend. If you think your child is so aggressive others don't like her, or if, on the other hand, she's so withdrawn at school that nobody even notices she's there, she could use some help learning to be a friend. This isn't done by throwing big, fancy parties, or by buying an expensive gizmo so other kids' jealousy drives them to seek her company. It's done by engaging your child's own personal resources—listening, sharing, taking turns, contributing to a group, and paying attention to others' feelings—so that other kids feel comfortable around her and even seek her out.

Alert

> Being a friend doesn't mean being a pushover. Social skills should be well-rounded and based on assertiveness rather than aggressiveness or passiveness. Help your child understand now, before middle school, that just as she can't make others do her bidding, neither should she do what other kids tell her if it's not good for her.

If you haven't done so already, teach your child about empathy: seeing things from others' perspectives. You can do this in subtle ways, for instance, by pointing out how an older person with a cane might have trouble opening the door at the bank, and asking your child to think about what she would do if she had to struggle with a cane and a heavy door. If she ignores you, ask her if she would appreciate someone opening the door for her, if she were in that situation. Over the course of a few weeks, these prompts will help your child realize how others feel, and this will make it harder for her to hurt others. In fact, it may even prompt your child to do good works, like opening a door for someone who can't. Positive role modeling on your part is the most powerful way to prompt good works.

In addition, she'll need to reach out to others by offering to share, to take turns, to invite others to participate in games and social activities. Ask your child who, if anyone, she'd like to spend more time with, and then take action to help her facilitate this, by allowing her to invite a friend over to play, by offering to buy Valentine's Day cards, or by bringing an extra popsicle, set of goggles, or scooter that she can offer to share when she goes to social events. If your child says she doesn't want to spend time with anyone, provide these opportunities for a few months, as it may turn out to be more fun than she'd expected. If you think your child is being picked on or this strategy doesn't work out, you can drop it or try it in a new environment where she doesn't have a "history."

The Real Meaning of Leadership

Children who have a strong need for power and control may try to make friends by dominating others with the mistaken notion that everyone will admire how tough and fearless they are. In middle school and high school among a group of similarly aggressive friends, this can definitely be the case and may have violent outcomes. However, most children in grade school aren't savvy enough yet to start a "crime ring," and this strategy backfires on them. Instead of liking them, other kids do what they say out of fear.

If you think your child craves admiration and recognition, brainstorm some healthy activities she can be engaged in that have a high chance of success. Even if they aren't to your tastes, try to find a way she can get connected to healthy interests of her own.

Next, have a conversation about leadership. Ask your child who she admires and who her heroes or role models are, and why. This can be a very telling conversation, and you can use this information to channel your child's energies in a healthy direction. If your child admires a role model you find appropriate, help her learn more about the role model; if your child admires a role model you are uncomfortable with, ask more about why and see if you can point out the same admirable traits in other, healthier role models. Finally, it's important to show your child that a successful leader is usually someone who helps others get what *they* want, rather than someone who uses others for her own benefit. Successful leaders—

and this is even more important in the twenty-first century—are humble, wise, and caring, and make those around them feel good about themselves. That's why people follow them.

How to Bond and Create a Secure Environment

With each passing year, you become more of a facilitator and less of a direct provider to your child. Now that your child is in grade school, you are still the most important adult in his life, but you're behind the scenes—where once you were the co-star, now you're the director. Facilitating with grace and wisdom isn't easy, but with a few tips you can transition smoothly so your child shines on the stage of his life.

Low Pressure

While you're emphasizing empathy and rolling out rules, your child needs less academic and athletic pressure, not more. If you're concerned about a behavior problem, improving it should take priority over grades and extracurricular performance, and you should never insist on winning at sports but on the fun of improving as an individual and the spirit of being on a team.

 Essential

Remember, extracurricular activities are important, but not crucial. You can drop out for a season while you and your family focus on behavior, emotions, and bonding so your child can operate from a strong base. Extracurricular activities will have more meaning when your child feels safe at home and school and strongly attached to you.

What you *can* insist on is your child completing homework, attending school, and letting you know if he has trouble with a particular assignment or subject. Reward improvements: if your child had an F in math last time, but this report card shows a C, that's cause for recognition, praise, and reward, not grumbling about how the child could have gotten a B or an A.

Trust

During the grade school years, it's also important to develop a strong sense of trust, to really ingrain it in you and your child's relationship before middle school and peer pressure begin. This means loosening the reins little by little and giving your child the chance to tiptoe out into life, come back, and tiptoe out again, a little farther each time. Each time your child ventures out—say, joining a new activity, or walking to a friend's house after school, check in and see how it went, and talk over what happened with your child so you're an active participant. By being actively involved, you'll be more capable of making small corrections if things go a direction you don't like, instead of having to make huge interventions. You and your child will trust each other more.

How to Have a Dialogue with Your Five-to-Ten-Year-Old

Your child's conscience is well-developed now, and she can use logic more easily, even several steps of it, to solve problems, make judgments, and determine the likely outcome of her or others' actions. Capitalize on her ability to think through problems during these years.

Communicating Your Values

If you want your child to grow up to be a well-rounded, balanced individual, make sure that her life and schedule reflect that. Favorite pastimes and hobbies are important, but if you only push your child in one area—say, academic performance, or piano lessons, or baseball—you risk your child losing out on the chance to develop other skills. And there may be other skills that, had she the opportunity to develop them, she might like even more than what you've already signed her up for. So don't force her to pick one sport or hobby and stick with it for life; give her the chance to mix it up from season to season. Your child is also old enough for community involvement: have her participate in a holiday food or toy drive for needy families, volunteer at an animal shelter, or help an elderly neighbor water plants or carry in groceries.

In addition, you should continue to have conversations that focus on empathy and point out that some rules aren't *your* rules, they're the world's rules. Now that your child is old enough to read, ask *her* to stop and read the signs at the airport, in the rec center, and at the movies. This makes compliance easier and your child more aware of her place in the world.

Being a Role Model

Of course, the single most important thing you can do to communicate your values to your child is to model them. As Gandhi said: "Be the change you wish to see in the world." You have to be the change you wish to see in your child, a much smaller, yet more powerful undertaking.

 Fact

Childhood obesity is a global pandemic, with millions of children around the world—at higher rates in first-world countries—overweight or obese. Adults aren't faring much better. Obesity has lifelong health implications, including a shortened life expectancy, so help your child to take steps now to stay healthy.

For example, if you want your child to get daily exercise, stop eating junk food, and live a healthy lifestyle, you will have to take the first step. If you want your child to be polite to others and consider their feelings, you'll need to do the same. If you want your child to spend less time plugged into gizmos and consuming media, you'll need to show how important this is to you by doing so yourself. Being a strong role model and admirable force in your child's life will give your child a real-world hero, so maybe in a future conversation about heroes, you'll be the star!

Sample Reward-Rule-Consequence Scenarios

Now you can put these concepts into action for five-to-ten-year-olds. You'll still need to focus primarily on rewards, and you can now assign your child responsibilities that are a little more difficult or require more mental effort to remember and carry out.

How to Reward Good Behavior

A star chart is still effective, though you might want to change the look of it, or ask the child to decorate it himself. If your child isn't excited by stickers, use check marks on a dry-erase board. You'll find that kids this age are more motivated by adding up small "points" and cashing them in, rather than by getting a Lego or other small toy each time. Still, don't make the prizes too big—staying up fifteen minutes later or getting thirty extra minutes of screen time are ample prizes for ten or so points. Competition is a huge motivator at this age, so your child may also be motivated to compete with himself by beating last week's total points for an additional prize.

Start the chart by choosing two to three good behaviors you want to encourage, such as completing homework each night so that he gets into the habit of doing schoolwork and having to harness his potential. Even if assignments are too "boring," or just for "dumb kids," reward him for doing them. You might also choose to reward acts of kindness toward other family members. Tell your child the rewards are effective immediately, and post them in a conspicuous place. Finally, don't check out once the program is set up; remain actively involved because your child still needs verbal praise, affection, and hugs from you for motivation.

How to Decrease Problem Behavior

As always, try as much as possible to reframe problem behavior so you're asking your child to *do* something instead of to *not* do it. However, there will be negative behaviors, such as destroying property, failing to do schoolwork, and lying, that need consequences

Time out is still effective at this age, but you might want to call it something that sounds more age-appropriate, like the "cooldown zone." Also effective is the incremental loss of privileges, *if* it's done in predictable chunks, instead of randomly or sweeping, which can infuriate a child because it seems arbitrary and unfair. So, delineate this ahead of time, write it up, and present it to your child by saying something like, "Here's the first rule. 'No destroying others' property.' What kinds of actions do you think are considered destroying property?" Give your child a chance to name some, like breaking a sibling's toy, punching holes in the walls, or whacking things with a stick. If the child stays silent, throw out a few examples yourself, then point to the rule chart and continue: "If you do this, here's the consequence. 'Miss the next day of soccer.' That could be soccer practice or a soccer game, whichever is coming up." Tell your child the rules are effective immediately, and post them in a conspicuous place.

CHAPTER 12

Parenting the Defiant Middle-Schooler

Most parents and teachers dread the middle school years because of their storminess and children's vulnerability to peer pressure on every issue from choosing a favorite band to using drugs. "Wait!" parents often think, "My kid is too young to be dealing with these issues! I thought these problems wouldn't start until high school!" Yet middle school is often the time you'll get your first chance at dealing with what you thought you'd see in high school.

Middle Schoolers and Defiance

As your child matures, a little more defiance of authority is normal. Adolescents are becoming their own people, and that means flexing their independence "muscles." Yet just as with every other age group, you keep normal defiant behavior normal by responding to it appropriately, rather than shrugging it off.

Inside the Middle School Mind

Puberty is the biggest change that kids go through during the middle school years. Before middle school, they're innocent little kids; afterward, they're adolescents, and they are more than just physically sexual, they are capable of understanding sexuality as well. Who helps them understand sexuality is up to you—either you can give your child the correct information, or you can wait until peers and the Internet educate your child. Remember that most twenty-first century teens will see online porn, and confront this head-on by making sure your child gets the correct information about both the physical act and the emotional and physical consequences. Finally, talking about sex should not be a one-time occurrence, however uncomfortable. Revisit the topic with a little more information from time to time.

Kids also grow more conscious and aware during the middle school years. You can no longer have an adult conversation right in front of your kid, using a certain tone of voice that will just fly over her head, the way you can with smaller children. Where once your child could have picked up on just the emotional cues of financial stress, marital tension, and worrisome world events, now your child becomes fully conscious of these heavy issues around her. If your child hears about any of these issues, don't ignore how it can affect her, and offer comfort and an opportunity to talk.

Why Middle Schoolers Defy Parents

All of childhood is a push-pull exercise between kids and their parents, and this becomes extremely apparent during the middle school and high school years, when kids act independent one minute and then come running into your arms another. Be patient, and give the child a safe harbor whenever she needs it.

Your middle schooler will defy you at some point during these years as she learns what kinds of behaviors are appropriate and desirable now that she's able to control more of them herself. Think of it like learning to drive a car: you've been watching someone else drive smoothly along, and then you get your first crack at it, and you weave all over the road and jerk forward and jerk to a stop, then stall. It takes awhile before you can get your own driving to go as smoothly as your teacher's. As your child learns to navigate the world, she'll go too far at times, and at others, not far enough. She'll make big mistakes. Just make sure you're in the passenger's seat to get her back on the road when she starts to veer off course.

What You May Be Experiencing

Suddenly, the smooth sailing is over, and you've hit stormy parenting seas, with increased technology and media consumption as the sandbars that pop up unexpectedly on your radar screen. You may be experiencing some of the following behaviors and defiant situations.

Peer Pressure

You probably remember this one from your own childhood. Suddenly, your rules and expectations are constantly compared to those of your child's friends and their families. Your child does things you think are clearly not "him," or that strike you as stupid or confusing, since he's known all his life that trying alcohol or going somewhere without telling you is against the rules. What happened? Peer pressure is probably a contributing factor, and you can deal with it, but not stop it.

 Essential

You can give your child some freedom from peer pressure by offering to be the bad guy. You can give your kid permission to use "My mom won't let me," or "My dad said I have to be home by five," as excuses for any activity he doesn't want to engage in.

You can't control peer pressure, but you can use it to your advantage by surrounding your child with positive peer influences. Some ways to give your child alternate peer environments could be going to church or temple, visiting family, or allowing your child to find and join a club based on art or self-expression, like dance or photography, where the tone might be calmer and the social standards different from those at school. These experiences could bring your child huge relief if peer pressure at school has been heavy, and your child needs a break from pressure to be violent, wear the right brand of jeans, or listen to a particular kind of music.

Where Is My Kid?

Your child goes to school all day, then to an extracurricular activity, and you see him during dinner before he does homework or has screen time; on the weekends, he wants to be immersed in his social and extracurricular life. If in the toddler years you were the costar, and in the grade school years you were the director, now you've become executive producer—you might offer input and advice that shapes the production, but you're not present for every shot.

To remain a force in your child's life, you must be sure to have regular emotional contact with him. Five-minute freezes and bonding are necessary; eating together at least once a day without the interruption of phones and television is also extremely beneficial. It's also important to decide which occasions you allow your child's friends to share—inviting a friend to a party or the beach is wonderful and necessary, but there should also be family-only times, when your family is alone together and friends are not invited.

Signs That Something Is Wrong

Kids at this age are testy and defiant, and the changes they go through may make even the most normal, even-keeled kid seem out of sorts and grumpy. However, there are specific problems that can contribute to defiant behavior, and markers you can use to identify real problems.

Depression

Depression is a common problem—affecting people of all ages, all across the globe, at surprisingly high rates. In fact, nearly a quarter of women will suffer from depression at some point, and about 17 percent of the general population will experience it. If your middle schooler appears sad, withdrawn, restless, fatigued, has changes in eating or sleeping patterns not attributable to a growth spurt, or seems tearful or irritable, she could be depressed. Any talk about suicide should be taken seriously and the child immediately connected to a therapist; explicitly tell the therapist that the child spoke about or seems fixated on suicide.

Teasing, Bullying, and Exclusion

It's painful to see the child you love be a "loner," or be excluded from a clique or activities that she's dying to be part of. It's hard to see the quirks and beautiful qualities that make your child unique be targeted by kids you think are just jealous, or who are suffering from issues of their own. And it's even harder to explain that this won't matter in a few years to a kid who's dying to be "cool" if she's been deemed "uncool."

 Alert

A word of caution: some experts recommend enrolling a child in karate or another self-defense sport to beef up self-confidence and give the child tools to fight back, if necessary. However, if your child is being picked on and labeled a "wimp"—especially if he is a small, sensitive boy—and you add to this by pushing for sports, it could backfire and make your child feel even more alone and depressed.

If your child is reluctant to go to school, ride the bus, or engage in activities she used to enjoy, consider that she might be being picked on in one (or more) of these environments. Kids tend to hide this information from parents because parents usually react by charging down to the school or calling the principal, embarrassing the kid and making the situation worse in their kid's eyes. If your child has been physically assaulted, you *should* contact the school or police. Finally, though there's no excuse for bullying, consider if there is a particular differentiating characteristic that makes your child a target: middle schoolers with disabilities or weight problems, or who may be homosexual, are often singled out. Give your child lots of love and affirmation, ask about how the child feels about the attributes that make her different, and put your child in alternate environments where she isn't so different, like those mentioned earlier in this chapter.

The Markers

When you don't see your child as often as you'd like, you may know something's bothering her but not know what or whether it's normal adolescent angst or cause for concern. If your child seems down in the dumps for a day, you should respond with concern and let her know you care. But when should you pay special attention? When should you dig deeper to find out if it's something serious?

In general, the following symptoms are indicative of a range of serious underlying problems—from depression to dating violence to drug use and more—that you should try to understand when they persist over a few weeks or more, or when they steadily get worse:

- Abrupt changes in sleeping patterns and appetite (not attributable to a growth spurt)
- Abrupt changes in behavior, or changes in personality
- Abrupt changes in friends
- Reluctance to engage in activities formerly enjoyed
- Difficulty concentrating
- Marked decline in school performance
- Irritability
- Unexplained aches and pains
- Unexplained injuries
- Self-inflicted injuries, such as cutting
- Reckless behaviors
- Tearfulness and frequent crying
- Lack of motivation

- Reluctance to go to school
- Restlessness, agitation
- Mood swings (not attributable to hormones)
- Withdrawal
- Strange giddiness or hyperactivity
- Crime
- The homicidal triad (see Chapter 11)
- Reference to or fixation on troublesome behaviors, such as suicide or drug use

Middle Schoolers and ODD

By now, you've probably become familiar with the major signs of ODD: loss of temper, arguments with adults, active defiance of rules and requests, anger, resentment, spitefulness, vindictiveness, being deliberately annoying toward others, being easily annoyed by others, and blaming of others for misbehavior, all over a period of about six months or more. You probably also know how to look out for signs of developing CD. Following are the special considerations for ODD in the middle school years.

It's Everybody Else's Fault

The last two behaviors listed above—being easily annoyed by others and blaming others for misbehavior—are particularly evident in middle schoolers with ODD. Using their new powers of logic and reason, tweens and even teens will often blame aggressive, defiant, even violent behavior on authorities whose fault it is for being too bossy or strict, or on other kids who are just getting what they deserve for being annoying, stupid, or some other insulting label. If your kid's logic sounds reasonable, you might be tempted to believe that authority *is* actually the cause of the behavior, not a possible cure for it. While it's fair to consider rules and adapt them for your child's increasing maturity, make changes carefully, and don't throw rules out the window as this could likely result in further defiance.

The Problem with Isolation

If your middle schooler is isolated because he's a loner or because you keep him at home away from others, the lack of social life could make him more resentful and defiant toward you and other authorities. Though a tween's social life is full of land mines, it's a necessary component for healthy development. Make sure your teen has a reasonable amount of freedom for his social life and that you nurture it with the same care and attention you nurture his physical and cognitive growth.

How to Be a Cool Parent— But Mostly a Parent

Your kid wants to be cool, and to be cool, everything in his life must be cool-ified, including his parents. Keep in mind that no matter how much you "coolify" yourself, you and your rules would still be a source of squirming embarrassment for your middle schooler. Here's how to keep your child healthy without going down in the middle school Hall of Shame.

Should You Be Your Child's Friend?

No. Kids might think they want this, but they don't, and if you are willing to be a middle schooler's dream parent, you might be doing so for your own self-esteem or need to revisit your own middle school years, rather than out of concern for your child.

Alert

If you *are* grappling with your own self-esteem or your need to revisit the middle school years, take a step back for self-analysis and even a few therapy sessions. It will serve your child best if you keep your own needs out of your parenting.

The fact is, your child can and will make lots of friends in life. She can't go out and make more parents. *The parents have to be the parents* for the child to develop normally and to feel safe and secure. So have fun together, bond together, and be a part of your child's life, but don't forget that you are the parent and you—and no one else—are charged with the raising of your child. It's her only chance.

But Everybody Else Gets to Do It! Coping with Peer Pressure

There are two ways to cope with peer pressure. The first way is to actively discuss the issue with your child on a frequent basis. When "everybody" else gets to go to an unsupervised party, get a new gizmo, wear clothes that look like lingerie, or stay out until 2 A.M., you can say, "I love you too much to let you do . . . ." As your child matures, you'll need to add an explanation so it doesn't sound arbitrary or unfair: "I love you too much to let you do . . . because that usually leads to . . . and if that happens you could be hurt or end up feeling bad about yourself. So no, you can't do that." Explain your own thought process and logic; it's interesting to a kid who's developing her own. If your child argues, listen, and unless new information is added, such as the party will be supervised or the clothes won't be worn to school, say, "Thanks for sharing that with me. I've heard what you said: that . . . , but it's still not going to happen."

The second way to cope with peer pressure is to help your child's self-esteem and positive self-concept. Encourage her endeavors, nurture her unique qualities, surround her with the alternate peer environments, and shine the light on others who have overcome peer pressure to live healthy, fulfilling lives. You might find these examples in adolescent self-help books, in the alternate peer environments, during your bonding activities, or in your immediate and extended family. The alternate environments will also diminish the impact of the dominant peer group, which are school friends.

How to Bond and Create a Secure Environment

Speaking of bonding, you can do it effectively with your middle schooler. Whether you're baking cookies, following a GPS treasure hunt, or taking up mountain biking, your child's maturity makes it possible to do new, fun things and to also give him some supervised control that will help validate him as a trustworthy, maturing person.

Your Child in Charge

One way to bond with tweens is to give them new responsibilities that are more than just chores: responsibilities that require thought, planning, and choice. Give your child some training on cooking, then ask him to make dinner once a week. If your child wants to baby-sit to earn extra money, support this with praise and a crash course (your own or a paid class at a YMCA or other facility) on how to be safe.

When chores do have to be boring, see if you can infuse them with the opportunities for thought, planning, and choice that motivate the maturing child. So, if your child has to mow the lawn, put him in charge of checking the gas can the night before to make sure it's full, and let him have some say in the types of plants you have along the border. If your child has to do the dishes, as long as they're cleaned, don't micromanage the chore and ignore—or affirm—his way of doing things, even if it drives you crazy. Letting your child take on responsibilities will ease the load on you and also help him feel proud of the trust you have in him, thereby improving your relationship.

Controversy and Quiet

Now that your child is aware of the world around him, expose him to both the controversy and chaos in the world as well as the quiet and peace we need to be healthy. First, don't ignore or shy away from uncomfortable or controversial subjects. This means more than gritting your teeth for "the sex talk," it means asking his opinion on issues close to his heart like the school's tardy policy, as well as some he may not have considered, like the death penalty. Listen to his opinions instead and ask him to consider other points of view, rather than jumping up on a soapbox.

 Essential

Buying print paper, magazines, and books and leaving them lying around is a way to jump-start conversations. Once your kids are in middle school, let them know that the reading materials in the home are open to them, and when you see them reading, ask what they're reading and what they think.

This information should be tempered with times for peace and quiet. In order to be healthy, we all must tune out the terrible goings-on in the world for a few minutes each day. Your home is also a safe harbor, a place where you and your middle schooler can learn new recipes, play catch, walk the dog, listen to music, do home repairs, and pray, meditate, or relax together. There has to be some downtime built into your lives, a time when it's okay to wake up a little later, wander around in your pajamas, and not have every moment of your time regimented and scheduled.

How to Have a Dialogue with Your Middle-Schooler

These bonding activities are the perfect moments to have a dialogue with your middle schooler that will keep you informed about what her friends are doing, what's cool, how to use the new lingo, and most of all, how to protect her effectively.

Decoy Activities

Much of the time, with tweens and teens, you have to strategize to get an effective conversation, as anyone knows who's asked a teen what she did that day! If you want your kid to say more to you than "Fine," "Nothing," "Nobody," and "I don't know," direct questions aren't as effective as using bonding activities as decoys for conversation opportunities. Instead of saying, "Let's talk about school, drugs, your friends, and what we can do about peer pressure," try, "Let's go shopping," "I need you to help me clean out the garage," or "Do you want to go fishing?" Once you're engaged in the activity, keep relatively quiet, and allow plenty of time for your child to think up a topic of conversation and lead the way. Then follow.

How to React

At some point during one of these conversations, you're likely to hear something that gets you upset, such as references to drugs, alcohol, sex, or other unsupervised, reckless behaviors and the people who engage in them, whether it's a new clique you're wary of or a music artist you can't stand. When you hear these references, don't butt in and say, "That person is an idiot!" or "I never want to hear you talk about that again!" Instead, when your child is *not* in direct danger, say something like, "That song talks about a crack whore. What do you think that means?" or "How do you think your friend's older cousin paid for that new car? What do you think about that?"

If your child *is* in danger, or would be if the circumstances happen again, you'll have to take the "I love you too much to let you do . . ." tactic. React calmly, thoughtfully, and honestly, and be sure to show both your concern and your love. Say something like, "I'm glad you told me about this. *You did the right thing, and I am so proud of you for being brave enough to let me know about it.* What you're describing here is a very dangerous situation, because . . . could happen in a case like this. I love you too much to let you be in a situation like that again, so I can't let you . . . anymore." Let your partner know about the situation, and if reasonable, solicit your child's input about how to avoid it happening again. You may also wish to educate your child on the subject by getting a book about it and reading it together.

Communicating Your Values

Instead of being shocked and baffled by heavy issues in your tween's life, steel your nerves and think of the middle school years as the training ground for similar issues in high school. Your child's personality is apparent, but will still be malleable for years to come, and you can have a lasting, positive effect on his values and sense of right and wrong. As always, be the change you wish to see in your child by modeling appropriate behaviors.

Boundaries

A social life may be the ultimate motivation for a tween, so it's the perfect time to teach your child about friendships, including how close is too close. You can "coolify" boundaries somewhat—though right now it will never be cool enough—by explaining that each family or home is like a special club, and no matter how many other good friends your family has, nobody else is a member of the club.

Fact

> Boundaries are hard because your child desperately wants to be a member of the cool kids club, and will want friends involved in every aspect of life that you allow. However, you'll undermine the child's emotional stability, not to mention your family stability, if you don't teach and enforce boundaries.

Begin by explaining what's off-limits for you personally: how much money people make, how much they weigh, personal identifiable information like social security numbers, sharing sexuality with anyone other than the doctor and a spouse or partner. You neither show nor tell other people about such personal subjects, nor do you ask them to show or tell you. Next, explain why it's important to keep these things private: because people can use information like this to hurt you, so you can only trust members of your club with it. Ask your child which of these items are applicable in junior high, and if there are any more he has to add. Then explain that people who repeatedly try to violate your boundaries cannot be trusted and should not be included in your lives. Finally, while you can and should include your child's friends in many activities, you must also insist that some activities are for members only.

Teach Your Child How to Think

By explaining things like how you choose friends and enforce your personal boundaries, you're sharing crucial thought processes with your child that can become powerful tools for navigating life. Explaining that you make decisions by thinking through possible outcomes of your actions before selecting the one you think is best, is extremely helpful and can also improve your relationship with your child. Say something like, "I'm going to stop for gas now instead of later because the gas station is right next to the road I'm on. If I waited until we got to the next off-ramp, where I know that the gas station is several blocks away, it would be less convenient." This teaches your child how to arrive at logical conclusions and also makes life appear more orderly to him, instead of living in a chaotic world where grown-ups make arbitrary decisions just because they feel like it.

Sample Reward-Rule-Consequence Scenarios

Now you can put these concepts into practice for your middle schooler. You should continue to focus primarily on rewards; rewards can be more abstract and earned over a greater period of time now. Once you have gotten the most important defiant behaviors under control, your child should be assigned several age-appropriate household responsibilities.

How to Reward Good Behavior

Contrary to what she may say, a middle schooler still wants love, praise, and affection from her parents, so when your tween does something right, something you want to encourage, let her know. Comments like, "Way to go!" "I'm proud of you," and "I knew you could do it!" will make her swell with pride on the inside, even if what she says is, "So what?" or the famous middle school refrain, "You're *embarrassing* me!"

Reward charts should be revamped with a less juvenile look, and should be focused on fifteen-minute increments of screen time, later bedtime on weekend nights, or, better yet, a reward your child helps select. Some behaviors you might want to list on the reward chart are, "Calling Mom every day after school to check in," or "Being at school on time." Remember not to take away any check marks once they're earned, and write out the rewards explicitly so your child doesn't get into a hair-splitting argument later. As your child grows older, you may find that the rewards and rules must be extremely explicit and sound longer than is reasonable; that's okay, just make sure that you and your child agree they're clear.

How to Decrease Problem Behaviors

Be just as explicit outlining the rules against problem behaviors: "You must be home fifteen minutes after school ends on days you don't have drama club and fifteen minutes after drama club ends on days you do have drama club, unless Mom or Dad gives you permission before school starts that day, or you will lose fifteen minutes of screen time." Again, enlist your child's help in choosing consequences for problem behaviors. You can ask, "What kind of punishment or consequence do you think would stop you from doing X?" Tell your child that the rules are effective immediately, and post them in a conspicuous place.

CHAPTER 13

Parenting the Defiant Teen

The teen years are finally here, and most parents wish there was a magic remote control so they could rewind to the grade school years, or fast-forward to college. Being the parent of a teen is an exercise in grace, in letting go in small steps and trying not to say, "I told you so," when things go wrong. In the next section, you'll learn something about teens that will dissolve some of the mystery and frustration associated with parenting them.

Teens and Defiance

As with all the other phases of childhood, some defiance is a normal part of teen behavior. A child displays most normal defiance during the toddler and teen years. What causes this? Why do teenagers sometimes seem so blockheaded?

Inside the Teen Mind

Have you ever seen the bumper sticker that says, "Attention teenagers! Quick—leave home while you still know everything!" or heard people complaining about the thick-headedness of teens? There's a good reason for this: physical maturity is complete before mental maturity. If you're frustrated with your teen, it may help to know that even though you have this apparently full-grown person in your home—someone who's capable of driving a car, pushing a lawn mower, holding down a job, being sexually active—the kid's brain is not done developing. Teens are capable of rational thought, but they can't always map out consequences of their behaviors. That leads them to act impulsively and do things that seem, well, stupid.

 Fact

> Incidentally, maturing physically before maturing cognitively has helped the human race reproduce. Teens are capable of having sex before they are capable of thinking through the consequences of sex. If it were the other way around—if you could understand sexuality and its consequences before you were sexually mature—there would be fewer teen pregnancies, and probably fewer humans.

You'll probably be less frustrated with your teen if you remember that she is not yet cognitively mature, and that you need to help her become so. Before she does something "stupid" (that is, something that *seems* stupid to an adult who has a better ability to grasp probable outcomes), stop her and prompt her to start thinking about consequences. You can ask, "What do you think about driving without a seatbelt? What do you think might happen?" or "Okay, I hear you say you don't want to go to college. Can you add up how much money you would make working at the surf shop or phone store or McDonald's per month, and how much your expenses would be if you lived on your own?" Involve your teen in cognitive processes instead of jumping straight to the conclusion and insulting the teen with, "That's stupid! Why aren't you *thinking*?"

Teens and Defiance

As you've read, quite a bit of defiance is normal in teens. That's because teens are carving out their identity and defining themselves both as individuals and as members of their peer group, whether that peer group is the punk rock girls at school, the Sims players online, or vegetarians in general. It makes teens feel very good to stand up and say, "Hello, world! This is who I am!" even if they don't really know who they are yet. Expect your teen to "try on" several different identities before she finds the right fit. Carving out an identity as an individual also means gaining independence, so you'll have battles over things like curfew, screen time, freedom, and such issues as whether music with suicidal overtones is against the rules.

Rites of Passage

Teens need some recognition for their coming of age. The introduction of this book explained that the absence of a larger "tribal" family unit might make it more difficult for parents to cope with defiance. It can also do away with the rites of passage humanity has often celebrated throughout history, and which help people feel comfortable about having new roles in different phases of life. These days you aren't going to send your son out into the forest for a week or announce the onset of your daughter's menstruation with a big party (she's probably grateful to be spared this).

While some religions and cultures still do celebrate bar/bat mitzvahs, first communions, and *quinceañeras*, mainstream Western culture has lost many of its rite of passage rituals, so you'll need to recognize your child's step-by-step maturity with increased privileges, responsibilities, and lots of love and affirmation. You might find your teen will be proud and more pleasant to live with if you recognize her not just for her accomplishments, but for her coming of age in various steps: starting high school, learning to drive, getting a driver's license, making a varsity team, being in a college-prep course, graduating from high school, and so on.

What You May Be Experiencing

There are some teens who aren't defiant, or hardly ever are. If you've seen another family with model teenagers and are wondering why your life can't be as peaceful and placid as the parents of those kids, take heart. What you're going through is not unusual, and when it gets bad, there are things you can do and places you can go for help.

Testing the Limits

You set up rules and agree on them with your teen—rules that seem totally fair to everyone, such as an 11:00 curfew on Friday nights. And then, later that week, your son comes home at 11:10 and as you're about to dole out the consequences, he says it was the fault of his friend, who was driving and couldn't find his keys. Or, you tell your daughter she is not allowed to go to so-and-so's house, and she calls you to tell you that now that she's in the car with her friends, *they* have decided they are going to go to so-and-so's house, and she is stuck with them and they're on their way, so she just wanted to let you know.

 Essential

> When you hand your teen the rules, make it clear that you will enforce them whether his friends cooperate or not. Your teen must learn, by practicing, how to speak up and get out of a social situation because he has another obligation. This will be a helpful skill later.

Rules are rules. Teens have a tendency to look for loopholes and to try to get off scot-free by blaming their friends or outside forces when they disobey. Teens will test the limits not because they are dead-set on coming home at 11:10 or dying to go to so-and-so's house, but because they are determined to see if you will stick to the limits. So do. If you ever allow an exception, be sure of two things: it is a special circumstance far beyond the teen's control and which is unlikely to recur (i.e., a car accident), and your teen will test the limits to find out if you will make exceptions for other rules.

Warped Perspective

You only have to flip through a magazine or visit a stock photography website to see that teens are usually portrayed as sullen thugs who sit next to spray-painted brick walls in baggy or goth clothes with enough facial piercings to pick up radio frequencies. Obviously, most people don't think teens are as cute as toddlers. Do you think that's fair? Turn the tables: do *you* like teen music that always portrays grown-ups as pushy jerks who hate fun and squelch self-expression? A change of perspective might help you get along better with your teen. Step back from what the media says about teens in general and think about *your* teen: what is wonderful, lovable, and amazing about *her*? It might help if you saw her teen years as another magical phase in growing up, one that you get to witness and cherish.

Signs That Something Is Wrong

In Appendix A, you will find a list called "The Markers." "The Markers" are behaviors that can be indicative of a wide range of serious problems, from depression to drug use to suicidal tendencies. This list is applicable to the teen years as well. Read the list and keep it in mind as you parent during the teen years so you know when your teen might need serious help. In addition, consider the following two markers for the teen years.

The Mouth Speaks from the Heart

While middle school or younger children are usually just parroting the speech they hear in the media or from friends, teens who talk about drugs, sex, violence, and other serious problems are giving you a big clue as to what they're doing or considering doing. If you hear your child using drug culture slang, talking about how much he loves guns and how he thinks movies that show people getting blown up are cool, or suddenly is having a new awareness and focus on stalking, take note.

Alert

If your child talks about suicide, indicates that he'd like to blow people up and has access to a weapon, *call a therapist immediately*. If you think your child is at risk of harming himself or others, don't wait for the bonding activities described below; act immediately.

Ask your child more about his friends and interests, ramp up the bonding activities, and employ some decoy activities as explained in the previous chapter to try to get a better feel for what's going on in your child's life and whether you need to intervene. Sometimes, your presence and involvement in his life will provide adequate protection from other, more harmful activities; other times, you may need to call a therapist.

When You're Out of Touch

Another red flag is not having a good idea of what's going on in your teen's life or who his friends are. If you realize that you don't know whether your teen is talking about real friends or media characters, if you can't remember what's on his schedule for a given day of the week, or if you don't know who his teachers are and how he's doing in school, it's time to get more involved in your teen's life. If that's a big change, he'll probably resist it at first and it may be uncomfortable and awkward for both of you. Do it anyway. Use decoy activities; take your teen out to eat, offer to let his friends come over (when you will be home), and show up to watch games or school performances, even if your teen says they're unimportant.

Teens and ODD

What's the difference between normal teen behavior, or "teenager-itis," and behavior that's cause for concern? In addition, you now know that just because a behavior is within normal ranges doesn't mean it should be ignored, so how do you handle both normal defiance and worrisome defiant behaviors?

How Far Is Too Far?

ODD in teens is "teenager-itis" taken to the extreme. All teens, including teens with ODD, will push the limits; teens with ODD will push the limits excessively, so much that others are hurt (physically or emotionally) or property is destroyed at home, school, or in other environments. A teen with ODD will probably be extremely defensive and frustrated about other comorbidities, such as anxiety, depression, or a learning disorder, and may try awkwardly to articulate these frustrations, insulting or cursing at you at home, in front of others, or in therapy. Review the symptoms of ODD and CD and ask a therapist for an evaluation if you suspect either of these disorders.

Remorse

Another red flag of ODD in teens is lack of remorse. The teen with ODD will push limits to the extreme, hurting others as a result, and then seem not to care, or to even be happy with the outcome. If your child says things like, "So what?" "It serves her right," or "Good, I'm glad!" after hurting other people, or if she simply seems not to care, she may have ODD. If your child seems to have hardly any emotions—no remorse after hurting someone, no excitement after achieving a goal, no sadness after a tragic event—a state called "flat affect" by psychologists, your child may have experienced some trauma and could benefit from the help of a therapist.

How to Bond and Create a Secure Environment

In general, you need to remain present in your teen's life no matter how much he pushes you away. Be there, and be aware. Your presence in your teen's life builds his trust in you and keeps you in the know about what he's up to, good or bad, so you can protect and celebrate him at the right times.

The Dos

Involve your teen in household chores and responsibilities. Make time for bonding activities, and take turns choosing what you'll do. Model the behavior you want to see in your kids. Use decoy activities primarily as an opportunity to listen, and secondarily as an opportunity to talk.

 Question

How do I listen so he'll talk?
A helpful tip is to wait ten seconds before speaking. This will accomplish two things: you'll be able to edit what you say before you say it; and it gives your teen a chance to add more information that might be important.

Be clear and consistent with rules and consequences. Show your teen love, give him praise for what he does right, and follow through on rewards. Show up for sports events, school performances, and recitals, and nurture his interests by helping him find activities and possible careers in fields he likes. Require school attendance and homework completion. Help his brain develop by prompting him to think through the possible consequences of his behavior before acting.

The Don'ts

Don't bail your child out of responsibility for his actions; if he gets in trouble at school for failing to turn in homework, don't step in and make excuses. Don't criticize, label, judge, or insult your teen, his friends, or his pop culture idols. Don't let him drink, do drugs, or have sex in your home with the faulty logic that at least you're there and can supervise if anything "goes wrong." And never break the law with your child by drinking or using drugs together. You may be there supervising, but your supervision is worthless if you allow your teen to behave recklessly.

Don't allow endless free time, such as a whole summer without responsibilities or structure (instead, sign him up for volunteer work, a job, fun classes at a community center or arts program, or summer school at the high school or junior college). Don't ignore your teen and assume that everything will be okay. Don't give up on your child by sending him away to a radical wilderness program, a convent, or an old aunt's house in another state when his behavior gets wild. Don't believe that "scared straight," or boot camp-style discipline programs work, because they usually backfire. Don't call the police on your child unless every other method of discipline has been tried and hasn't gotten results.

How to Have a Dialogue with Your Teen

Do your conversations with your teen feel one-sided? You ask, "How was your day? What did you learn? Who is that guy you were kissing?" and your teen answers, "Fine. Nothing. Nobody." This type of exchange is extremely frustrating to a parent who wants to be part of a teen's life and know more about what's going on, but there are better ways than question-and-answer to stay in touch, even if your questions are the open-ended type that get longer responses from adults and small children.

Conversation Tips

Put more thought into setting up an *opportunity for conversation* than you do into what types of questions you want to ask. When your kids are in the car with you, prohibit anyone (especially yourself) from answering a cell phone. Play a pointless card game with your teen, or offer to help her find more information on activities and fields of study that interest her. Avoid TV, but agree to go to a movie that requires you to drive together to the theater, or surf the web together so you can talk about the things you see online and what websites she likes.

During these interactions, let your child be the star of the conversation, and follow her lead, and you will learn more about her. Offer up your own opinions, advice, and stories from your youth very infrequently, or only when your child asks (which will probably be infrequently). When you do have something to say, count to ten before jumping in so that your child has a chance to finish speaking, and you have a chance to make a calm, well-thought-out statement or question.

Responding to Teen Criticism

Teens are often highly critical of their parents, sneering and groaning about Mom's hairstyle, Dad's huffing-puffing morning jog, the music their parents listen to, the friends they have, their boring idea of fun, and even the way they read parenting books about how to deal with teens. Insults are normal, but are inappropriate and should not be tolerated; criticism can sometimes be reframed in a low-key way using the communication skills in Chapter 8: "It sounds like you don't like my shirt, huh? But *I* do, because I feel comfortable in it and I think it makes me look thinner than I am."

If your child says, "I can't believe you're such a lousy parent that you can't even deal with me without reading a book about it!" you can respond with the truth, which is, "I'm glad you noticed. I'm reading this book because I love you and want to be the best parent I can for you. There's always something new I can learn."

Communicating Your Values

How do you communicate your values to your teen? Isn't it a given that the "biggies"—drugs, sex, alcohol, and other reckless behaviors—are off limits? There are only so many ways (and times) you can say "Don't do drugs." But there are other things you can do.

Modeling and Honesty

Just as at any other time in your child's life, you need to model the behaviors you'd like to encourage. Teens are very perceptive, so make sure what you say matches up with what you do, even if your teen isn't around. If you drink and drive and think your kid won't know, you're running the risk of your child finding out, copying the behavior, and seeing an example of your dishonesty.

Teens will often try to find cracks in their parents' perfect facades by saying such things as, "Oh, so *you* never had sex before you got married?" or "Sure, like you never tried alcohol before *you* were twenty-one." Take note: this is the rare invitation for *you* to do the talking rather than listening and waiting for your teen to open up. Rather than lying or using smoke-and-mirrors, tell your teen the truth about what you did . . . and how it affected you at the time and in the future.

 **Question**

How much detail should you include?
Enough to tell the story, but not enough to teach your child how to engage in the behavior. If your teen seems very interested in say, how you rolled a joint, respond with, "You don't need to know the details. The point is that I did it and I'll always regret it because . . . ."

It's important to include the repercussions of your behavior in the story because, remember, teens are not quite able to figure out these long-lasting implications for themselves. You can say something like, "I'm so glad I didn't have unprotected sex. Two weeks after she broke up with me, my high school girlfriend got pregnant by another guy, and he ended up having to quit school to get a job and raise a family."

Well-Rounded Teens

Teens need a mix of scheduled activities to keep them stimulated, and unstructured free time for thinking, creativity, and a social life. Unless your family particularly needs the money, consider prohibiting your teen from getting a part-time job and instead using his time for an activity that builds life and career skills, such as an internship or volunteer position. This is much more valuable than learning to waitress or fold clothes for what amounts to a few hundred bucks—unless you think your teen needs to realize how poorly unskilled jobs pay and how hard it is to be on one's feet for an eight-hour shift. In the end, a teen needs to be well-rounded, with more in life than just school and the Internet, so find other interests and nurture them.

The Importance of Image and Friends

Image and friends are extremely important to teens and often drive their parents nuts. When should you put your foot down about music, clothes, and friends that are potentially harmful? What's the best way to get cooperation? Before you haul your child onto a talk show for a teen makeover that won't stick, consider these more effective tips.

What to Do if You Disapprove of Music

Telling your teen that a particular song or artist is completely off-limits is probably ineffective. Twenty years ago, your own mother could take away your cassette or CD and that would be that. Today, your child can just download another copy, or get a copy on a friend's computer, and it will probably cost a whole ninety-nine cents, if anything. So the best way to deal with music you find offensive is by first asking your child more about the artist and the lyrics.

She may not have even stopped to listen to the lyrics if the tune is catchy enough and the vocals obscured by other instruments, so give her the chance to think about it. Then ask her opinion: "How do you think that singer feels about black people/women/white people?" Second, find an upcoming opportunity for balancing input—if the song seems racist, look for a museum exhibit, movie, or cultural event to go to together that throws light on the race in question so your daughter can draw her own conclusions.

What to Do if You Disapprove of Clothing

Clothing is an area where you can effectively make rules, but choose your battles. It will be most effective if you do so beforehand, by making the rules and presenting them *before* your son is walking out the door late with his pants around his knees. You can effectively make rules about decency (e.g., no private parts showing, always wear underwear, only the waistband can show) and courtesy (no offensive T-shirts, dressing appropriately for the occasion). You'll get the best results if you work on this with your teen and are extremely literal, so don't be surprised if you find yourself in a hair-splitting discussion of exactly how many inches from the belly button your daughter's pants can be. Tell your kids that their image teaches people how to treat them, so if they dress like their body is available for anyone to touch, even the people they don't like will think they can touch it. Finally, don't buy clothes you don't approve of.

What to Do if You Disapprove of Friends

This is the toughest of the three issues because your child will probably care most about it and fight hardest for it. If your child has a friend you just can't stand because he's obnoxious, don't mention it. If your child has a friend you think is a shady character but you don't know why, ask your child more about the friend, and ramp up the bonding activities and decoy activities to learn more.

Alert

> There may be a friend who is dangerous or harmful. It isn't easy to enforce, but you can forbid your child from seeing that person outside of school by saying, "So-and-so is obviously very interested in drugs and is probably using or selling them," and then using the "I love you too much to let you . . ." formula.

You may cringe at the idea of spending more time with people you find obnoxious or suspicious, but inviting your child's friends to your home or along for an outing from time to time can be helpful. By welcoming all but the most dangerous or harmful friends, you get to supervise, learn more about your kid, and sometimes even channel their energy into something constructive by dropping them off at the skate park or offering them twenty bucks to wash your car.

Sex, Drugs, and Alcohol

By now, you have learned many skills for how to get in touch with your child, talk about important issues, and make effective rules. While you can't *ensure* your child won't try drugs or have sex early, you can make it more unlikely by using some of these tips.

Behavior Contracts

You can use a behavior contract whether or not your child has already engaged in the behavior. The contract should have two components: a literal explanation of what you're agreeing on (no drinking, for example), and a description of what will happen if your child breaks it (such as your child forfeits the car keys and must go to counseling once a week). It may be helpful to solicit your teen's feedback for what should happen if she breaks the contract.

Courage

They may be some of the scariest conversations you ever have with your child, but you *must* talk about sex, drugs, and alcohol with your teen. Don't be afraid of "messing up" or embarrassing your child because you probably won't mess up and probably will embarrass him, but you have to do it anyway or you're sending the message that either you don't care or are afraid of these issues. Teens still need your protection and need to know you care. No matter how much your child resists your love and attention, especially your desire to talk about important issues, stand firm. "Troublesome" teens who claim they don't need love or other people are those who need it most.

Sample Reward-Rule-Consequence Scenarios

It's time to put rewards, rules, and consequences into action for the teen. Don't forget to look for what your teen does *right* and reward and praise it. Your teen should also have clear, explicit rules and a firm understanding of what will happen if they're broken.

How to Reward Good Behavior

As noted earlier, the most troublesome teens are those who need the most love and affirmation from adults, especially their parents. Even teens who insist they don't need you to love them anymore need it, and if your teen is defiant and out-of-control, you need to get in touch with your love for him despite your frustration.

Also keep a reward chart that looks mature (you'll probably need to lose the stickers and get a black magic marker instead) and is focused on accumulating points for good behaviors that add up to a larger reward. Find your child's interests and use them as rewards: increments of screen time and time out on weekend nights are big ones, so might be use of the car or a day trip to someplace he's always wanted to go. Don't make the rewards so big they are hard to earn, or so expensive or inconvenient that you can't deliver, or your teen will be frustrated, resentful, and more defiant.

How to Decrease Problem Behaviors

If your teen is at all cooperative, enlist his help in outlining the rules and consequences. This may be a long conversation, so plan time for it. Ask, "What kinds of rules do you think are fair? What should we all do to live here happily and peacefully?" and "What kinds of consequences do you think would stop you from doing . . . ?" Again, expect your teen to need you to be extremely literal and specific, so it's okay if your rule is a long, long sentence instead of just a simple "No breaking things." Consequences should be easy to enforce, so if you are not home in the afternoons, you can't expect to enforce a "no screen time" consequence.

Your teen may also want to counter with some rules of his own, such as "I want you to stop nagging me." If you are having a calm, constructive conversation, and the request is reasonable and can be defined in a behavior-specific way (for example, rephrasing "No nagging" as "If you are exactly on time I won't comment on how you were almost late."), consider accepting your child's requests. If your conversation is volatile and the requests unreasonable, say, "It sounds like you're looking for some fairness. I'm willing to consider following some of your rules, too. We can talk tomorrow when we're calmer. It would help if you write down some of your suggestions ahead of time." Showing you are fair and not making rules just because you're on a power trip will likely get you more cooperation and peace.

CHAPTER 14

Treatment for Defiance

There are many methods for treating defiance, some tried-and-true, others innovative, some highly effective and others less effective or even damaging. Chapters 3 and 4 gave you some basic information on medical and psychological treatment options. Here is more in-depth information.

Medical Interventions

If you have not already taken your child for an exam or screening to rule out an underlying medical problem, re-read Chapter 3. In brief, there are many medical and development reasons that could contribute to defiant behavior, including autism and diabetes, and a thorough screening by a pediatrician or pediatric specialist is important to rule out other factors.

Treating Medically Based Mental Health Problems

After a comprehensive screening has been completed and you find that your child has a medical or developmental problem contributing to defiant behavior, be sure to ask the specialist about the best way to treat it, and for referrals to experienced treatment professionals. A child psychiatrist will likely be your best bet for treating a child with medically based mental health problems, since psychiatrists are MDs and can prescribe medications.

Alternative Medicine

There is little evidence that alternative therapies like acupuncture have a positive effect on defiant behavior; however, if they appeal to you, it is fine to try them as long as you advise your other treatment professionals (such as the psychiatrist) of your full treatment plan. Some homeopathic doctors prescribe supplements, which, while based on natural products, are quite potent, and should not be taken until you've consulted the professional in charge of the child's treatment.

 Fact

Exercise improves mood. While it's not exactly therapy, getting your child out of doors for fresh air, running around, and burning off energy will improve her mood and keep her from bouncing off the walls. If you live in an area where playing outside is not safe, take her to someplace she can play after school or on weekends.

There is anecdotal evidence that massage improves mood. While this has not been documented extensively, there is a belief that massage can help "smooth out" an angry kid just as it soothes adults. Search for "therapeutic massage" in a phonebook or online and explain to the therapist that you are looking for a soothing massage for a minor before booking the appointment.

Counseling and Psychotherapy

It seems that counseling or psychotherapy is recommended for just about every modern ailment. What is therapy, what's so great about it, and what can you expect to get from it?

What Is Therapy?

Therapy is treatment for behavior, thoughts, and emotions in an interpersonal relationship with the practitioner. There are many different schools of therapy; what you are likely to find today is a combination of approaches. Most therapists will spend some time learning more about the client and the factors, both internal and external, that are causing the immediate problems in her life. The client will also get a chance to "unload" and speak freely to a neutral third party about what's bothering her. Next, the therapist will spend some time with the client working through those issues and teaching her practical solutions, such as changing thought processes. This takes time, practice, and follow-through. Finally, the therapist will evaluate the treatment for effectiveness and recommend any necessary next steps.

If your child is in therapy, she will not be lying on a leather couch staring up at the ceiling and talking about Oedipus. Therapists who work with children adapt their practices to make them age-appropriate. Small children may play with puppets, draw with crayons, or engage in other "play" that helps them articulate their feelings and describe the stressors in their life. Older children may be asked to read an age-appropriate book on their own or with the therapist, or select a figurine that speaks to them and describe to the therapist how it relates to their life. If your child needs to be in therapy, you can prepare her by saying, "You know what the doctor is, right? The doctor helps your body stay healthy. Well, a therapist is a special kind of doctor for your feelings, and you can talk about any feeling you have, like feeling sad or worried, with the therapist."

Therapy Options and Scenarios

Most likely, a therapist will recommend that you attend therapy as well. In an ideal world, the child would be in individual therapy, the parent(s) would be in individual therapy and possibly marriage counseling, and the whole family would come in for group counseling. However, this would be logistically difficult, exhausting, and probably quite expensive.

A more realistic solution is to seek education and strategies through a parenting support group (usually available through a therapist or hospital), enroll the child in therapy once a week or once every other week with a therapist who will give you updates after each session, and enroll in family therapy on the odd weeks.

Medications

Medicating kids for behavioral problems is a hot-button issue. Is medication effective at helping kids, or is it just "big pharma" trying to maximize profits? Can you trust that medication will help your child?

How Medication Can Help

Medications can be extremely effective at improving a child's mood and behavior. If your child is so angry or anxious he can't function or get along with people, short-term medication has the advantage of providing the necessary "breathing room" for learning new behaviors and employing other, more long-lasting solutions.

A child with ADHD may benefit from medication that helps him pay attention in school so he can do better and be less frustrated. A child who has alienated potential friends can have a chance, through medication, to build social skills and learn how much fun it is to have friends, motivating him to continue friendly behaviors and forming habits that can be built on later, after medication is tapered off. Similarly, if a child is depressed and suicidal, medication can elevate his mood, decreasing the chance of suicide; meanwhile, the child can undergo therapy and learn to cope with the trauma and other factors in his life that have led him to become so depressed.

If your child is going to need long-term medication for a mental health condition that is unlikely to improve through therapy or by ignoring the problem, talk with the psychiatrist about your child's condition and educate yourself fully about what you can expect long-term. There is no cure for some types of disorders, and medication is the only option that can help a person lead a full life.

Cautionary Statements

However, there is a great deal of distrust today in psychiatric medications, because kids are often misdiagnosed and wrongly or overly medicated. To decrease the chance that this will happen to your child, be sure that the treating professional knows the full scope of what's been happening in your child's life, and work with a professional you trust and who seems to be paying attention to you and your child. Only a child psychiatrist should prescribe psychiatric medications to a child; a pediatrician does not spend enough time evaluating the child to make an accurate psychiatric evaluation and prescription.

 Alert

Do not take your child off psychiatric medications or tinker with the dosage without consulting the psychiatrist. Sudden withdrawal from some psychiatric medications can cause death. If you would like to decrease or stop medication, or if you can't fill the next prescription because you'll be on vacation or can't pay for it, consult with the psychiatrist first.

In addition, very few psychiatric medications have been evaluated and approved by the FDA for use on children. If your child's psychiatrist suggests medication, ask if you can have a conversation with her about the diagnosis, prognosis, and why a particular medication is recommended. Ask how long it will take before you notice a change in behavior. Ask about the side effects and cost. Ask if there are any warning signs to look for, because some depression medications have a worsening effect in kids, and can actually darken their mood instead of lighten it. Finally, if your child will need medication, tell your child that you love him and want the best for him, and that you and the doctor believe that the medication will help him feel more comfortable.

Boot Camps

You've probably seen "get tough" boot camps on TV talk shows or reality programming. They show how "problem" kids with bad attitudes and usually lazy dispositions lace up combat boots, crumble and cry in front of oppressive camp leaders, tromp through brush and rocks to build fences or go on quests, and come out of the program tougher, wiser, and more respectful. It's an effect created for entertainment purposes, and it doesn't work.

Did You Know . . . ?

Did you know that boot camp-style programs are largely undocumented, unregulated, and run by unlicensed professionals? That's right. If you dig deep enough, you will probably find that the only programs that are documented and run by licensed professionals are government-run, and are usually mandatory care facilities for children who have been removed from their homes or who are in a kind of halfway house after leaving juvenile hall.

If you voluntarily send your child away to a boot camp, don't expect the results you've seen on television, where producers and writers script what will happen so that viewers can have a sense of triumph when a mean bully gets what he has coming. The ends of these programs are tied up as neatly as thirty-minute sitcoms, but most people know that life doesn't work that way. *You* are your child's parent and the only one who can protect her. When she's away at an extended care facility, you don't know what types of dangers she'll confront—violent peers, unclean conditions, abusive or deviant leaders—and no one will have her best interests at heart the way you would at home. Because of this, *boot camps usually make behavior worse* as your child tries to fend for herself among violent and aggressive peers and leaders.

What Your Child Learns from Boot Camp

Voluntarily sending a child away to boot camp, or any place you can't care for her daily, tells her two things: you have given up on her, and you don't care about her and want her out of your life. She'll see you as weaker than she is and lose respect for you. It also teaches her that violence, aggression, and force are the only way to get things done, because that's how boot camps operate. Finally, it teaches her not to trust anyone and to remain emotionally detached, because people who supposedly love her can ditch her at any time.

If you are considering boot camp because you must remove your child from a dangerous peer group for an extended period of time, it would be much more effective for your whole family to go to a specialty camp on parenting skills and relationship improvement. You could use this time to bond and to show your child that, rather than abandoning her, you are right there beside her during the hardest times. You may even consider moving, which is expensive and inconvenient, but will be much better for your family than sending your child away.

Other Professional Interventions

There are other professional interventions that may come across your radar screen. Here's what you can expect from each of these types of interventions, including what works, what doesn't, and how to tell the difference before you sign up.

Classes and Support Groups

You may consider enrolling yourself or your child or both of you in a class or support group. In general, whenever you consider a treatment option, try to determine if the option has been proven effective. Organized, regulated programs usually have to document their progress if they want to continue receiving funding, so ask to see what their results have been in past years.

 **Essential**

"Recidivism" (ruh-SID-uh-VIZM) is a term you may come across. Recidivism is the repetition of undesired behaviors after a person has been trained to stop them or has been released from treatment. You can ask a program coordinator about "rates of recidivism" to learn if the kids in their program improved or not.

Classes and support groups should be run by a licensed professional and consist of an organized curriculum or meeting format. A group of angry teens watching movies on Monday nights in a church basement with a well-meaning but unlicensed recovered criminal is a recipe for disaster—your child could actually learn how to be *more* defiant and find a peer group that reinforces the undesirable behaviors. Look for a program run by a hospital or clinic that is managed by a licensed and experienced psychotherapist or counselor who is present during the sessions.

Circles of Shame

Once in awhile, you'll find a type of intervention in which the offender is asked to be present with victims or people he has hurt, usually by sitting with them in a circle. This session is run like a ritual, with a leader controlling aspects of the environment such as lighting, seating, and noise levels. Victims get a chance to tell the offender directly how much they've been hurt, and the offender is supposed to listen and realize the extent of his actions.

This type of program appeals to victims and victim advocates as it helps victims recover from grief; however, it is not effective at stopping the offender's behavior. If anything, public shaming, embarrassment, and exposure makes the offending person angrier, more frustrated, and with a need to exert even more control over his life, which could result in more aggression. If this is not part of your heritage, it's probably best to forego it. If it is part of your cultural tradition, ask your elders to consider that it could make your child angrier and he could hurt someone else as a result, and ask if there are any other ways you can approach the situation.

What to Do about Relapses

Relapses are normal; expect them. No one is perfect, including you, your therapist, and your child, and forming new habits is difficult. If you expect relapses, you'll know how to prepare for them, what to do when they happen, and how to win the war instead of the battle.

Identifying Relapse Factors

There are two categories of factors that can contribute to a relapse: immediate factors, such as high-risk situations and poor coping skills, and underlying factors, such as a family's lifestyle and the child's ingrained habits. If you would like to minimize the likelihood of a relapse, you should identify and sandbag these cracks in the dam.

To identify immediate factors, ask yourself the following questions: Are there situations that trigger your child's defiant behavior, such as playing violent videogames or changing plans at the last minute? If so, how can you minimize them? Does your child have difficulty changing tasks or dealing with frustration? If so, help him overcome these difficulties by explaining how you adapt, teaching him to do the same, and helping him stay calm in the face of difficulties and surmount them one step at a time. Does your child have a skewed belief that defiance will actually get him what he wants and make him happy? If so, gently remind him how this has backfired in the past and will probably backfire in the future.

Fact

The Relapse Prevention Model, primarily developed by psychologist G. Alan Marlatt, was originally applied to helping prevent relapse in alcoholics and drug addicts. Part of the theory states that seemingly small changes can have large effects, and it can be applied to prevention in almost any ingrained habit, including defiant behavior.

To identify underlying factors, you may need to talk with a neutral third party you trust, such as a therapist, to gain a broader perspective about what could contribute to a relapse in behavior. Be prepared—this might be uncomfortable for you, as you might hear that your family's lifestyle and the behavior you're modeling are contributing factors. Are you willing to change your behavior? Are you willing to patiently help your child learn new habits? If not, you will probably see more of the same. A therapist can help you with these difficult tasks.

Taking Action

Again, you must identify the factors, and you must also alert your child to these high-risk situations that trigger undesirable behavior. For example, if turning off the TV usually results in a tantrum, you can say, "You can watch TV now, but at 5:30, we'll be turning it off. Have you noticed that sometimes that's hard for you?" or "I know you are often frustrated when you're in a large group of kids and feel like no one listens to you. Do you want to practice being part of a team?"

Next, take action. Ask your child if she would prefer to skip watching TV tonight, or if there's another way you can avoid the trigger, such as a two-minute warning, or turning the volume down slowly or muting the TV, and *then* turning it off so the change is not so sudden. Talk about this before the TV goes on. You may also want to practice how you'll turn the TV off before the desired program goes on, and reward your child with the small "peanuts" during this practice session so you can ingrain the desired behavior in a low-risk situation. It is perfectly fine and helpful to give your child rewards for practicing successfully in a low-risk situation.

Finally, you must build your child up with self-confidence and trust. It's helpful to say, "I believe in you and I think you can do it," but it's even more effective to give your child an example, however small, of how she's been successful at overcoming difficulties in the past. A child who has been in therapy, is on medications, or has become the center of adult stress and worry may not feel so hot about herself. Look for testaments to her personal strength and remind her of her accomplishments. You want her to move from "Mom believes in me and thinks I can do it" to "I believe in myself and I think I can do it."

CHAPTER 15

Dealing with a Crime

If your child is involved with criminal activity, it's important to be realistic about the situation—don't sweep a crime under the rug and assume your child would never do such a thing. On the other hand, don't blow things out of proportion or have an overwrought, knee-jerk emotional response. That makes it impossible for your child to confide in you about what has happened, and your child may provide you with details that are important to keeping her safe and preventing further crime. This chapter contains complete information on how to deal with a crime.

Law Enforcement's Perspective

Your child may not have a favorable impression of law enforcement; for that matter, you may not, either. How does the law enforcement community view kids and crime, what can you expect, and how should you interact with law enforcement officers if they tell you your child has been involved with criminal activity?

Do You Know the Law?

One of the first questions law enforcement officers ask parents is, "Do you know the law?" Of course no one can memorize every city code and regulation, but it is important to have a decent grasp of the laws that might affect your child. For example, what time is curfew in your city? What are the laws about loitering, littering, and vandalism? What is the minimum age for drinking and buying cigarettes, and what is the punishment for using a fake ID to get around age limits? What are the traffic laws, and is your child old enough to drive a car, with or without his friends? If you see your child or his friends involved with an activity you think is questionable, pull your child aside and learn about the rules together. Be sure to include the punishment in your research, as it may be much worse than being in time out or having screen time taken away.

A Knock on Your Door

Having a police officer bring your child home may be in the top ten of a parent's worst nightmares. However, according to Dr. Tod Burke, a former police officer who's now a tenured professor of criminology at Radford University in Radford, Virginia, if a police officer brings your child home or talks to you without arresting your child, it's an informal procedure which probably means he's cutting your child some slack. If a child is polite and cooperative with the officer instead of mouthing off, and if the officer hasn't already made an allowance for the child on other occasions, this is a likely scenario that allows your family to address the situation and move forward.

 Essential

Remember and refer to the homicidal triad from Chapter 11. If your child lights fires, wets the bed regularly past the age of six, and harms animals (including insects), take note and contact an experienced child psychologist immediately. Also take your child to a psychologist if you see escalating aggression, or defiant behavior spreading from one environment to another.

In order to get the best results in this situation, Dr. Burke recommends you thank the officer and ask him to give you as much detail as possible. Don't jump all over the officer or defend your child, just *listen*. Conversely, it won't help to side with the police officer and jump all over your child. Your goal in this interaction should be to get as much information as possible so that you have a clear and realistic picture of what happened. Keep your child present during this conversation, and ask your child in front of the officer if what the officer has said is true.

Making Positive Connections

Another goal of law enforcement is to make positive connections with kids *before* they need to enforce the law. Sound familiar? That's because it's similar to parent-child bonding activities that help decrease the likelihood of defiant behavior. It's always more beneficial to correct behavior through a positive existing relationship than by cracking down on someone you hardly know.

Law enforcement organizations across the country have established youth outreach programs to make positive connections with kids and create a favorable impression of law enforcement before kids become involved with crime. Lt. Gil Owens of the South Carolina Highway Patrol recently founded a program called Touching Another Generation (TAG). He and his seventy troopers each must make contact with at least four teens per month at a time when the teens are not in trouble, and in a nonintrusive way, so they reach more than 3,000 teens per year (note that this is an action-oriented plan that has measurable results within a timeline). When the troopers encounter teens in a casual interaction, they ask them if they wear their seatbelts, educate them about recent traffic fatality causes and statistics in their state, and ask if they can come speak to the teens' class, football team, or other organization. Lt. Owens says the goal of the program is to show teens that law enforcement isn't after them, and it has been effective at breaking barriers and getting local kids to be more responsive to law enforcement.

Crime and the Future

The justice system is softer on kids than on adults, believing—as most everyone does—that kids are more malleable than adults and will respond better to rehabilitation than adults. Lighter sentencing is not intended as a "get out of jail free card," but as an opportunity for correcting criminal behavior so that the child does not grow up to commit more crimes. That's what happens if juvenile crime goes undeterred—the child will continue breaking the law, and as an adult, will face stiffer penalties and a life with fewer opportunities for fulfillment, pleasure, and success. If you want your child to have a fulfilling adulthood, take action now.

Taking Action: What Should You Do?

It's no fun to face the fact that your child has committed a crime, and is much more difficult than being in denial. However, denial won't help your child and could actually make matters worse. For your child's sake, as well as the sake of those around her, you need to head off criminal behavior before it gets any worse, so here's how to handle matters at home.

Talking with Your Spouse

Talk with your spouse or partner as soon as you have suspicions or after a conversation with a law enforcement officer. Explain the situation and ask if your spouse knows of anything else that could help you understand the situation—perhaps your spouse saw your child's friends with cans of spray paint, or thought he smelled marijuana on your child, but pushed any suspicions away in the absence of other information. Two heads are better than one, so compare notes. Then, present a united front by agreeing on how you'll handle the situation so that your child knows *both* of you love her, but will not tolerate the behavior.

If You Suspect

If you suspect your child is involved with criminal activity, but don't have any evidence, you should have a conversation with your child that includes five things:

1. An affirmation of your love
2. A review of what you've found out
3. A statement of the law
4. A mutual discussion of how to resolve the problem
5. An explanation of accountability

 Alert

> Do not play detective and go through your child's room looking for evidence unless you need to for serious safety reasons, such as a strong suspicion that your child has a weapon. Violating your child's space undermines the trust in your relationship and will make communication harder and your child less receptive to what you say.

Here's a skeleton example of what you can say (if possible, you and your partner should both be present): "I love you very much [affirmation] and I'm worried about you because I've heard kids are drinking at your friend Kevin's house [review] which is against the law because they're under twenty-one [statement of the law]. What can you tell me about this situation? Do you have any ideas about how to stay safe in a situation where people are breaking the law like this? [mutual discussion]" Allow plenty of time for your child to respond and offer some ideas. If you think they're insincere, tell her that you don't believe her suggestions would be effective and ask if she has any more. Then say, "Remember that law enforcement considers this a crime, and they'll take it seriously. I do, too. I will check to see that we've resolved the problem, and if I find out you've been drinking or been around teens who are drinking, you will be grounded for two weeks and won't be allowed to go to Kevin's house anymore" (accountability).

If You Know

If you know your child has committed a crime, but law enforcement has not yet taken action, be proactive. Remember to talk to your spouse or partner immediately, and find out more about the crime and its consequences. Sit down with your spouse and child to discuss the problem, being sure to affirm your love for the child and explaining that breaking the law is serious and has consequences both at home and in the justice system. Make it very clear that you will not hide evidence, or contribute to the crime in any way.

If the crime is minor and no one has been hurt, find a way to resolve the problem without involving law enforcement. If the crime was major and/or someone was hurt, call an attorney to discuss your family's options. Finally, remember that honesty is a good policy, and it may help your child to turn herself in before law enforcement finds out, so remind her that this may be to her benefit and could help everyone involved heal before things get worse. If she does turn herself in, praise her highly for the courage and responsibility in doing so.

If Your Child Is Convicted of a Crime

If your child is convicted of a crime, you need to understand how your child views the situation, how to parent effectively around the situation, and how it can affect your child in the future. You also need to take specific actions as the parent.

Your To-Do List

At the top of your to-do list is affirming your love for your child. Though putting up a tough façade, and even possibly being thrilled by attention and drama, your child may be embarrassed to be involved with the justice system and scared of any potential consequences.

Tell your child you will be there for him no matter what happens, and that you will always love him, in good times and bad.

Next, call an attorney and discuss your options—as a juvenile, your child may have some options for rehabilitation and lighter sentencing. Your child's attitude is usually a big part of this, so involve your child in the phone calls and in-office meetings. Finally, keep the themes of responsibility, fairness, justice, and understanding in your conversations with your child. It is only fair that crime have consequences and that responsible parties own up to what they've done, and if there are any victims, educate your child about empathy using the tips in Chapter 8.

Understanding Remorse

Your child may express remorse after committing a crime, and you must discern whether it is remorse for the crime or for being caught. Find out by asking him how he thinks his actions have affected others. How does he think stealing makes a store owner or employee feel? How would he feel if someone pulled a knife on *him*? If he expresses empathy, he is probably remorseful about the crime; if he says, "Serves them right," or "Sounds fine to me," he is probably remorseful about being caught.

 Question

What is my child's attitude?
Your child's attitude is very important in healing after this experience and in working with law enforcement and the justice system. Remorse, embarrassment, empathy, honesty, and a willingness to cooperate improve your child's chances for rehabilitation. Mouthing off, being tough, or being combative or dishonest with law enforcement will make things worse.

It's important to know which type of remorse your child expresses because it is a good indicator of the likelihood of his repeating the behavior. Saying "I'm sorry" is a good start, but if he is sorry only that he got caught, expect that he has learned a lesson about how to cover up his crimes. Do not trust him in the situation where the crime took place, and reduce his free time.

The Role of Accomplice

Many times, a first crime is not the child's idea, but the idea of a more experienced friend—the first-time delinquent may be following along as an accomplice. This is not a reason to excuse your child's behavior, engage in denial, or think that your child was an unwilling participant, and you should still utilize the other tips in this chapter about what to do and how to talk to your child. Additionally, you should address this with your child by explaining what an accomplice is and stating that your child did contribute to the crime, even if he was unwilling (your child may have been perfectly willing, though). Try to minimize your child's contact with the friend in question, and explain that the justice system will probably be harsher if your child were to engage in another crime. Solicit your child's input for righting any wrongs and minimizing the likelihood that the friend will use him as an accomplice in the future.

Labeling

Labeling a child a delinquent, bad person, troublemaker, or other harsh description is dangerous and can make behaviors worse. Remember from Chapter 8 that it is more effective to focus on actions than labels. What happens if others have put a negative label on your child? Once someone is caught, goes through the justice system, and is labeled, everyone knows about it and the label is pervasive; it affects his whole life. Curiously, people take ownership of the label they're given and run with it. "Oh, no, I've committed a crime!" becomes "I'm a criminal," which becomes, "Hey, you know what? I *am* a criminal and I'm a real bad dude, so watch out!" It becomes part of the person's identity. If your child has been labeled, counteract this by emphasizing good behaviors and affirming your unconditional love.

Gang Involvement

Gangs are present in most, if not all, major metropolitan areas today, and in many rural and suburban areas as well. Are they present in your community, and are they a factor in your child's life? Here is how to figure out what's going on, and what to do about it.

Is Your Child in a Gang?

Now that gang culture has pervaded mainstream culture, the "gangsta" look and attitude are visible in kids who aren't involved with gangs, so style of dress, music, race, and culture aren't enough for a basis of judgment. Pepe Montenegro is a former gang member who was rehabilitated as a teen, earned a master's degree in psychology, and now works as a counselor and gang outreach coordinator in public schools. Montenegro founded Gang Outreach Educational Strategies and Tactics (GOEST), and recommends taking a look around, educating yourself, and getting in touch with your child. What are your child's favorite movies, TV shows, music artists, and idols? What does that graffiti-like writing on his notebook mean, or the markings he's drawn on his body with felt pens or had tattooed on permanently? Ask him, talk about his interests. Show that you are involved and that you care.

 Fact

Gangsta style might be cool with nongang members, but some specific gangs do have color schemes they wear like uniforms. The colors vary from gang to gang and region to region. If you think your child's dress indicates gang involvement, find out what the gang colors are in your area by asking your child or law enforcement.

Next, find out what's going on at school and during your child's free time. Who are his friends, and are they involved with a gang? How are your child's grades? Gangs typically don't encourage conforming to "the system," and falling grades could be an indicator that your child is being educated by a gang instead, educated for a life in crime instead of employment. Talk to your child's teachers and require good grades from your child through your system of rewards, rules, and consequences. Does your child have unexplained cash or a car, or possess drugs? These can also indicate gang involvement.

How to Minimize Gang Involvement

According to Montenegro, if your child is in a gang, he already has enemies and will probably bring problems to the home that compromise everyone's safety. It isn't realistic to ask your child to renounce the gang, but you can minimize gang involvement. One of the most effective ways to do this is by moving as far away as possible, which is expensive, stressful, and difficult, but will cut ties with the gang. If that's not possible, you should fill some of your child's free time with other, supervised activities that give him hope for the future. If you ever are going to splurge in life, now is the time, so sign up your child for the art class he has wanted to take, or cut into your vacation time to bond more with your child and develop his interests. Show your child the possibility of life outside the community by taking a trip to a university, signing up for the tour, and scheduling meetings with departments in which your child may have an interest. Tell your child you love him, affirm his potential, and tell him he can be someone.

Next, ask your school or local law enforcement agency if there are any gang outreach programs available, and what the quality of the programs is. (As you learned in Chapter 14, only consider programs with proven track records run by licensed counselors.) Kids who idolize gang members may be shocked to hear from former gang members that the gang didn't fulfill their expectations and used them instead of rewarding them. Kids may also be sickened to see the level of permanent disability gang members experience after shootings.

 Alert

Gangs often have websites, are computer savvy, and trace phone calls, so, don't research gangs over the Internet, and don't call law enforcement from your home. Ask hypothetical questions about what "a parent" should do if her child "were to be" involved with a gang.

Finally, reevaluate your current approach to discipline. Parents often tell Montenegro, "What am I supposed to do? I yell at him already!" to which he responds, "Is it working?" "No," is the usual answer. "Then stop doing it," he tells parents. Find a new approach. Keep up positive activities and reinforcement, and check with community organizations to see if what you're doing has a proven track record with other families; if not, ask for help.

How to Heal Beyond the Law

Upholding the law and standing by any sentencing received from the justice system is only a small part of healing after your child commits a crime. You must hold your child accountable for her actions and be aware of how she thinks, feels, and acts in order to effectively prevent further crimes.

Types and Objectives of Punishment

According to Dr. Burke, there are four different types of punishment. Each has a different philosophy and objective:

- **Deterrence:** applied with the belief that an unpleasant consequence makes people think twice before repeating the behavior. This is most effective at stopping crime that is planned or premeditated. Sometimes the goal is to deter the individual from repeating the behavior; other times it is to deter others from engaging in a similar behavior.

- **Retribution:** an "eye for an eye, tooth for a tooth" punishment applied with the belief that offenders should suffer similarly to their victims.
- **Restitution:** applied with the belief that offenders should repay their victim's loss in money or services.
- **Rehabilitation:** used more frequently with juveniles, it is applied with the hopes of helping the person resolve comorbidities that may contribute to crime.

What type of punishment do you think would be most effective for your child? What do you think would keep her from repeating the behavior?

Prevention of Further Crimes

The importance of bonding can't be overstated. You will have the greatest impact on your child's behavior by being a positive force in her life. Make regular, positive one-on-one time with your child a priority to prevent further crime, help your child develop in healthy ways, and be aware of what's going on in your child's life so you know what to do when things are getting out of control.

Resources in Your Community

Most communities have youth outreach programs designed to minimize crime and help kids rehabilitate who have been on the wrong side of the law. Reach out, find out what they are, and sign up for any free programs *as long as they are run by licensed facilitators and have some kind of proven track record.* Ask for free or low-cost counseling; you may likely qualify. If you don't inquire, you won't know what's available.

How You Can Cope

Having your child involved with a crime is stressful, worrisome, and even embarrassing. How can you move forward as an individual so that you can become a better parent? Does it even matter? The answer is yes, and here's how to do it.

Learned Behaviors

Differential association is the theory that people learn criminal behavior from others. As a parent, it's natural to wonder what you did wrong and to blame yourself, and it's well worth exploring the question of how you and your family's lifestyle may have contributed to your child's behavior, especially if the crime in question closely mimics something you or your co-parent has done. However, it's important not to label yourself a bad person or terrible parent, because, as you've learned, labels are not helpful; a focus on behavior is. You may need to re-evaluate some of your own behaviors and think about what you can do to parent more effectively, but chances are, you can't do it alone.

Support and Counseling

Any feelings you have are valid. Now is a perfectly reasonable time to ask others for help, so ask your boss if you can take a week off, ask family members to help with chores or hassles, ask a friend if you can meet for a walk or a cup of coffee to talk about what's been on your mind. Then, get counseling. It is not possible to go it completely alone, and most people will understand and appreciate your attention to your child at this time, so reach out.

CHAPTER 16

Dealing with Siblings

The issues you're having with defiant behavior don't occur in a vacuum—there are a number of other factors that may need your attention, not the least of which is a sibling relationship. How should you approach defiant behavior relative to a sibling, whether the other child is having a behavioral issue at present or not, and what should you do if *both* of your children are exhibiting defiant behavior?

How Defiance Affects a Sibling

All of the tension and stress at home that stems from your defiant child's behavior can impact a sibling in negative ways. The child who doesn't have a significant behavior problem may feel left out, annoyed, or resentful to see the attention the other child is getting as a result of bad behavior. This can lead to obnoxious or unwanted behavior in the child you *aren't* focusing all your energy on, making you even more stressed and tired. Also, birth order comes into play in any sibling relationship.

Birth Order

For better or worse, the oldest child is a role model and leader for younger siblings. The oldest child, when troubled, may begin to act more like a baby, or to act the age of the younger sibling, especially if he wants to get some of the attention that the younger one is receiving. Behaving younger than one's age is called "regression."

The middle child is often a peacekeeper between the older and younger siblings. Middle children are often overlooked by the adults in their families, as attention is focused on the "firsts" of the older sibling and "cuteness" of the younger. Special attention should be paid to rewarding a middle child's good behavior.

The youngest child will usually imitate the behaviors of the older ones, even if the behavior is defiant. Younger children often elicit adult attention for being cute, and this can cause resentment in older siblings.

How the Nondefiant Sibling Feels and Acts

The nondefiant child may resent the attention you pay to your defiant child as you attempt to stop bad behavior. She may wonder what the point of being "good" is if it doesn't get her the attention that being "bad" gets her brother or sister. That's a valid point and very logical thinking, and it can lead to twice the problems when the child whose behavior has been just fine decides to devise some attention-getting antics of her own. Be sure to keep up bonding activities and positive reinforcement of desired behaviors in order to prevent this.

On the other hand, another child may see the defiant behavior in a sibling and think, "Wow, I have to be *extra* good to make up for my sister's rotten behavior." While this is very considerate, it's too much pressure for a child. The child may also feel isolated and wonder why he is different; he may also be ashamed of the family and wish for a "normal" one. Be sure to keep up the love and affection with the other child so that he doesn't feel abnormal or under pressure.

When There Is More than One Defiant Child

It's hard enough to deal with one defiant child, so what do you do when you've got your hands full with two defiant children? For starters, if you are married, you and your spouse must present a united front.

Nurture Your Marriage

In order to be a strong parenting team, you and your spouse need to do more than just agree on strategies. You need to be connected. That means you'll have to spend some time nurturing your marriage *without* parenting, by going on a walk, drive, date, or full-on weekend away just to be together without talking about the kids.

If it seems like you are being torn in a million different directions by a million urgent needs, you're not alone. Most parents today have trouble balancing work, family, love, and personal needs. To combat this, try two things: first, consider removing something unnecessary from your life. Second, start with small—but measurable—chunks of time devoted to each need. For example, you can set a goal of one coffee morning per month with your spouse.

The Family Team

Another way to deal with more than one defiant child is to celebrate your family unit, showing your kids that you're all in it together, for better or for worse. What is unique and special about your "team"? You can make this corny by nicknaming your car or house and having inside jokes, or spiritual by making a ritual of saying a blessing before dinner or praying before bed. You could also emphasize coziness by making time for special things that, include only your immediate family, from run-of-the-mill activities like cooking and cleaning to fun stuff like going swimming or building a collective display as explained in Chapter 8.

Cope

The last strategy for dealing with more than one defiant child is to cope. Use the business mantra of "work smarter, not harder." Rather than adding one more task to a mounting pile, take a step back and evaluate your life. What can you take off your plate? Is there any force that's draining you without giving anything back, like staying up too late or focusing on a manipulative adult relationship that's tearing you down? Is there a temporary situation that's exacerbating your kids' behavior, and if so, how, and how long can you hang on until you get added support? Who can provide support—a church, a partner, an extended family member, an employer, government programs, a close friend? Don't be ashamed—most people love to help as it makes them feel needed and useful.

Allies: How to Keep Your Children from Cooperating to Defy You

It's one thing if your children are defying you to compete with one another for your attention, but it's a whole new ball of wax when they gang up on you. If you sense this is happening, be frank with any co-parent about what's going on and the need to address it as a unit.

Double Time

Create separate rewards, rules, and consequences for each child so that each child is accountable for her own actions. You can include on the list that collusion results in a "double time" reward or punishment—they can earn twice the goodies for cooperating together, or lose twice the privileges for allying against you. When you enforce this, make it swift and include both kids instead of trying to sort through facts in a who-did-what interrogation.

Divide and Conquer

"Divide and conquer" is a strategy used to take away power from an enemy by breaking up the group's unity. You can use it with your kids—any time you think they're ganging up, separate them. In the moment, send them to separate areas of the house for time outs, and confiscate cell phones if they're using them to strategize against you. Over the long term, you may need to get them involved in separate activities if these strategies don't help.

How to Reduce Conflicts

Chances are, your children's defiant behavior and resentment will erupt into a fight sooner or later. Your children may also be likely to fight if they are struggling to find their own identities in a household where attention is uneven, where defiance is part of one child's identity, or where there are no consequences for fighting.

The "No Fighting" Rule

The best way to reduce fighting is to make fighting *strictly against the rules* with consequences you enforce immediately and consistently. If your children currently hit, kick, push, or otherwise use physical force against each other, focus your rules on getting them to solve conflicts without physical violence. If violence is not an issue, but screaming, insults, and name calling are driving you up the wall and hurting feelings, make this behavior against the rules using clear, specific language such as "No name calling," or "No yelling within six feet of another person."

The Power of Words

You can also reduce fighting by refraining from typecasting your children or comparing them (saying things like "Jeff is the good, studious one, and Mark is our athlete" or "We wish you could get good grades like your big sister" are recipes for sibling rivalry). Your child's own words are a tool as well—teach effective communication skills as outlined in Chapter 8 so that your children have another tool in their toolbox besides their fists and nasty remarks.

Structure Together, Structure Apart

If your children fight frequently, some structure and the adult supervision that goes with it may be helpful. A good mix of individual structured time and shared structured activities may help, so take a look at your children's schedules and think about what you can do to change them. Are they spending every minute of the day together, or do they only see each other in the mornings when they fight over the shower? Can you or your spouse start a new family ritual on Saturday mornings where the activity is predictable and a parent is present to intervene before conflicts get out of hand? Is one child locked into the demands of the other's special schedule, and could that child maybe get a special activity of his own?

How to Talk to One Sibling about the Other's Problem

It is extremely important for the health of your children's sibling relationship that you pay attention to how you speak about any behavioral problems, and that you don't make the defiance a big deal in the other child's eyes if or when it becomes abnormal. Here are some strategies for talking about a behavioral problem or other condition.

What to Say

Find a time to talk to the nondefiant child when the defiant child is *not* present. Start from a point of empathy for her feelings, such as, "I saw you crying when your brother slammed the door in your face earlier," or "I know it has been hard for you to see your sister getting so much attention lately," and then allow your child some time to respond. Instead of defending the defiant sibling's behavior, or your own actions, listen and validate her feelings.

Then, segue into an explanation that builds empathy for the other child, such as "I wanted to let you know that your sister has been having trouble with behaving. I think it really *is* hard for her to explain her feelings and behave appropriately." Next, explain that your actions are partly to protect the child: "But just because she is having trouble does *not* mean that it's okay for her to behave like she has been. So, I have been doing everything I can to help her learn how to stop doing this. It takes time, and it may seem like she's getting all the attention right now, but I haven't forgotten about you. I love you and want you to be happy and calm in our house, so that's why I've been paying so much attention to helping your sister improve her behavior."

 Alert

> At this point, your child may disclose something you weren't aware of. Siblings can be abusive toward each other, so be prepared to enlist a therapist to help a child who has been victimized or hurt longer than you thought or worse than you anticipated. Don't deny what your child discloses or jump to the other sibling's defense.

What Not to Say

Don't make the other child out to be brain damaged, horrible, or crazy. Don't use labels like "bad," "hard-headed," "stubborn," or "slow." Don't align yourself with the nondefiant child against the other, as if the two of you are "in the know" and the other is a silly fool that you roll your eyes about behind his back. Don't blame defiant behavior on your spouse or anyone else. Don't ignore the desired behaviors.

What to Do for the Child Without the Problem

It's no fun to be the child who is behaving just fine and see the sibling who's acting out get all the adult attention. It can be very discouraging to see adults set up a rewards system for a sibling who punches holes in walls when you haven't been rewarded for not *ever* doing it, and meanwhile, you have to defend yourself from angry outbursts. Other than the above explanations, how can you help the child who *doesn't* have the behavior problem?

Love, Attention, and Rewards

First, you *can* give the nondefiant sibling that reward for not punching holes in walls. During one of your conversations together, you can say, "I realize that you've been behaving yourself very well, and deserve a reward for that." You can invite the sibling for a bonding activity of his choice, or institute his own star chart. Be sure not to compare your children when doling out rewards, as this will increase antagonism. So such comments as, "See? Your sister earned *her* reward," should be off-limits.

Teaching Effective Interactions

Effective communication skills and an understanding of others' behavior are helpful skills for anyone, especially the sibling of a defiant child. Teach your nondefiant child the art of effective communication that is explained in Chapter 8, and help him recognize the body language, situational, and behavioral cues that lead to a defiant outburst so he can anticipate them and get out of the way.

 Essential

A child with sixth grade or higher reading skills may enjoy taking a look through *The Definitive Book of Body Language* by Barbara and Allan Pease. An entertaining read, it includes illustrations and spot-on "definitions" of different poses. The tools in the book can help your child recognize cues in the defiant sibling to anticipate and avoid outbursts.

Also, your other child may need some assertiveness training, which you can get from many books or therapists. He should learn how to be an equal and get what he wants without resorting to aggression. You've heard the expression "low man on the totem pole"—you need to level the totem pole so that no one is anyone else's subordinate.

The Star of His Own Show

Finally, celebrate the unique and valuable attributes of your nondefiant child—go beyond the traits "he's well-behaved, quiet, and a joy to have around." What else makes your child special? What skills, academic, athletic, artistic, social, or otherwise does your child possess that you can highlight and nurture? Find them and help foster them.

How to Foster Lifelong Love Between Siblings

Once you have their interactions somewhat smoothed out, raise the bar for your family and go beyond getting along: approach real affection. Siblings who love each other are important forces in each other's lives, probably for much longer than you will be yourself. The greatest gift you'll ever give your children is their siblings.

Unique and Valued Individuals

Earlier in the chapter, you learned how to create unity by ramping up the family "team spirit." This is extremely important, and so is recognizing that the team is made up of uniquely amazing individuals. Celebrate your children's individual differences without categorizing them, and bolster each one's self-esteem by paying meaningful compliments and giving appropriate, sincere praise for work well done.

Showcase Positive Attributes

Give each child a chance to watch the other excel. Be careful: make sure this isn't one-sided or malicious (again, don't say things like, "Well, I see *your brother* made time for his homework!"). For example, if your defiant child is really good at a sport, get her on a team and take the other to watch the games, and vice versa.

Reward Positive Interactions

Your children's relationship may be so strained that you're at a loss to find any positive interactions. If so, remember that in Chapter 5 you learned to start very small, using "peanuts" to lead the elephant through the zoo. Be on the lookout for positive interactions between your children, however small, that you can praise and reward, because it's one of the best ways to get them to cooperate. If you start small, they'll follow where you lead, and eventually you'll get them to the place you want to go.

CHAPTER 17

Working with
Your Child's School

A nother factor that may require your attention when dealing with a defiant child is the school environment. How does the school handle defiant behavior, and what can you do, from everyday check-ins to long-term advocacy, to get the best results for your child? Also, it's important for you to know your rights, the services provided, and when to take action if something goes wrong.

Understanding the School

Understanding your child's school—the teacher, the administration and staff, and the school's philosophy—is key to strategizing effective interactions and working with them on a variety of factors that may affect your child at school. The best way to work with the school is to appreciate the unique situation of each individual, and to treat them with respect and kindness.

The Teacher

It's no secret that teachers in most public schools, and many private schools as well, are overwhelmed and overworked just trying to meet the requirements of the curriculum with a growing number of students per class. You can see how dealing with behavioral issues can seem to some teachers a disruptive annoyance that is not the first item on their priority list. As long as the teacher has not been cruel, or has not singled your child out for some kind of punitive treatment, he is probably just trying to do the best he can to teach the content with the time and resources he has.

The Administration and Staff

Administration and staff can be a wonderful resource for parents who treat them as individual human beings instead of an impenetrable, depersonalized system. This can be tricky because that's often how the "behind the scenes" personnel appear to a parent who can't get what he wants and then wonders where all his tax dollars are going. It's important to understand that these people are also overworked and underpaid, and are in education because they care, not because they wanted to get rich. Administration and staff must operate under regulations set up by a school district or state law.

The School Philosophy

Every school (and school district) philosophy is different. Some schools are traditional with an emphasis on order, authority, and the three R's, while other schools operate with a newer philosophy that favors differentiated learning and pays close attention to interpersonal relationships. A balance of the two ideologies—one in which people's differences are celebrated and emotional connections are made, but in which learning is still the top priority—is ideal.

 Alert

Still other school districts' philosophies are built around achieving high scores on standardized testing; high scores may be a way of advertising the school and nearby real estate. Testing is required, but if prep time seems excessive, compare it to other districts to see if it's normal.

Also, school districts take many of their mandates from a school board, a panel elected by local citizens. Remember that these elected officials are *your* representatives, and part of their job is to field parent concerns and work directly with the superintendent to form new regulations. In some cities, board members are paid a small stipend; others receive no pay. In some cities, board members run unopposed because few people are interested in the job; in others, elections are hotly contested. No matter what the situation, you have a voice with school board members, but, as with teachers, administration, and staff, there are more and less effective ways to get what you want.

How to Get What You Want

When you are functioning as an individual parent, rather than as a part of an advocacy group, it's important to see the whole school system, but to approach the individual people working in it as human beings. Savvy is essential at times, but following the golden rule will probably get you more mileage.

Be Kind

Now that you know that the system is made up of individual human beings, the first and foremost way to get what you want from them is to be kind to them. Follow the golden rule, and treat them as you would want to be treated in your job by the people *you* come into contact with. It's hard, when you're a parent with a full plate and who's hurting because your child is hurting, but it's *extremely important* that you not come out swinging. If you're angry and attack others, they'll be defensive and uncooperative, so your child won't get as much help, and you'll get even angrier. Don't waste your energy on tactics that make the situation worse.

Be Proactive

Being kind doesn't mean being passive—you can advocate for your child with class and courtesy. In fact, according to Diana Dessery Hensley, a licensed educational psychologist in Orange County, California, being "a sweet pain in the side" is probably your best strategy. So, be proactive whenever a new situation comes up: when your child has a new teacher, new counselor, or starts in a new school, make contact first. Introduce yourself and invite communication by saying something like, "Hi, I'm . . . , so-and-so's Mom/Dad. Here's my cell phone number. I really want to be involved with my child's education/counseling, so if there's ever anything you need to discuss about my child, good or bad, just call me." Get on their radar screen in a nice way, and whenever possible, don't wait for a problem before you make your first appearance.

Be Receptive

When you are contacted about behavior, a health concern, or a possible learning disability, listen to what the person tells you without being defensive or dismissive. When the issue is behavior, get as many of the facts as possible, and listen calmly instead of coming to your child's rescue and excusing, rationalizing, or minimizing the behavior. Thank the person who contacted you, and say that you want to talk to your child and your partner, and that you'll be in touch to let the caller know how you'll address the behavior. Then do so, and uphold any consequences that come from the school.

 Fact

The professionals working in a school have a strong concept of normalcy for the age group they work with. They're educated and experienced, and if they tell you something is a cause for concern, it is in your child's best interest to take their point of view seriously.

If a learning disability or health issue is the concern, you should also listen calmly and gather as many facts as possible. Say something such as, "Can you tell me what you're seeing that's leading you to think ADHD is a possibility?" and don't negate her observations. After she has finished speaking, ask what comes next, if there is a nurse you can speak with, if she will refer the child for screening, or if a "study team" can take a closer look.

Know Your Rights

Finally, Dessery Hensley recommends you know your rights as a parent. "Parents have a lot of rights," she explains. You don't have to sign anything you don't agree with or accept a recommended treatment plan if it doesn't seem right to you; you can ask for resources for more information, for time to consider the recommendations and weigh your options, and for a second meeting. If you're at a meeting to discuss your child's needs, such as at an Individualized Education Plan (IEP) meeting, remember that *you're* part of the team, and you have a voice in what's going on. Of course, you do have the right to an attorney, but unless an egregious crime has been committed, announcing you're going to get a lawyer will put school personnel on the defensive. They'll put any extra effort into minding their p's and q's so they don't get sued, rather than putting extra effort into figuring out the best way to help your child.

If Something Is Wrong

You've learned about organic causes for defiant behavior in Chapters 1 and 3, and how best to address these health concerns at home. Now take a look at how these issues are identified, addressed, and hopefully resolved within the school system, and also some key points that have resolved many behavior and academic problems with a few simple screenings.

Vision and Hearing

Always rule out vision and hearing problems. Children may not realize they have a vision or hearing impairment. Trouble hearing and seeing can make school one big frustrating endeavor for a youngster, and remember that frustration can definitely factor into defiant behavior. Farsightedness can make reading and writing difficult; nearsightedness can make looking at the board difficult. Other problems like astigmatism or the failure of eyes to work together as a team (some examples are strabismus and amblyopia) could also be at play. Left untreated, some vision problems can get worse and can even result in vision loss.

 Alert

> Most schools offer vision and hearing screenings. These are designed to catch some, but not all, hearing and vision problems, and so are distinct from comprehensive exams. If you suspect a hearing or vision difficulty, ask for a referral to a specialist who can conduct a comprehensive exam.

Similar problems can arise with hearing difficulties. If your child exhibits defiant behavior and has trouble in school, a hearing difficulty that impedes learning could also be a root cause. As with vision problems, hearing difficulties left untreated can get worse. Rule out any vision and hearing problems as a first step toward resolving academic difficulties, and make sure your child gets a *comprehensive exam* if a screening doesn't turn up anything.

ADHD

Most teachers have a good idea of what ADHD is, and how to teach kids who have it. If the teacher brings up the possibility, or if you know your child has ADHD but doesn't seem to be getting help learning despite this disorder, establish a kind, proactive presence with the teacher as soon as possible and gather some information about what's going on in the classroom. Once you have a clear understanding, ask what sorts of strategies he can recommend to help your child learn and refrain from disrupting the rest of the class (this will be a prime concern for the teacher). Don't go around the teacher's back and speak with a principal or vice principal if the teacher is doing an effective job or making suggestions that are worth trying, as this could be awkward for the teacher and cause him to become resentful of you and your child.

Dysgraphia

Dysgraphia is a writing deficiency. Children without any type of neural trauma can be dysgraphic if they have difficulty writing legibly and correctly for their age despite thorough instruction. Dysgraphia is unrelated to reading ability; it's simply difficulty writing, although it can co-occur with other learning disabilities. If your child is dysgraphic, she may experience pain during writing, have trouble with small motor skills, grip her pencil incorrectly, refuse or drag her heels when faced with writing tasks, and have terrible penmanship. Adults with dysgraphia often cope by typing everything, but if your child doesn't have that opportunity in school, she may not have another way to cope. Ask for a screening.

Learning Disabilities and Special Needs

Learning disabilities and special needs can be a source of frustration and questions of self-worth for your child. If your child has preexisting special needs, make sure she has access to the facilities and interventions granted by the government, and use the "sweet pain in the side" strategy unless your child is being victimized by the teacher or school, or if other children's cruelty is going unchecked. If that's the case, see the section called "Being on Your Child's Side" below.

If some of the first, simple interventions you and a teacher propose don't work, it may be a sign your child has LD. Again, have a conversation with the teacher in which you ask what she's seeing in the classroom, and offer insights into your child's behavior at home that may be helpful in creating a bigger picture. Testing is crucial; you need an accurate assessment of what's wrong in order to develop an effective treatment plan. Request that your child be tested, and put your request in writing. It's kindest if you hand-deliver the paper to the teacher and explain that you'll also send a copy to the principal's office. Putting the request in writing will make it official, and if you hand-deliver it or give the teacher a heads-up, and you already have established a positive relationship, this request won't put her on the defensive. Finally, treatment plans, as you've read in other sections of this book, should be based on proven research.

If your child has other special needs such as a physical disability, frustration and questions of self-worth could be affecting school performance. You must still rule out vision and hearing problems, then consider the possibility of ADHD or LD. Then, make sure your child has the necessary tools and treatment plans for the best education possible, and continue to be a "sweet pain in the side" in order to make sure she has access to everything she needs. Remember that you have many rights as a parent! You're a member of the IEP team, and you have a voice in what the team decides. For more information, look at the book *Nolo's IEP Guide: Learning Disabilities* by Nolo Press.

Giftedness

The term "giftedness" has a positive connotation in most circles, and most parents whose children are gifted feel a sense of pride with this label. Yet because gifted children often have special academic and emotional needs, parenting a gifted child can be extremely difficult, and not all of the special needs are desirable or inevitably result in superstardom as the child matures. Gifted children are not necessarily good students; in fact, if they are not nurtured in their learning, they can become extremely frustrated and angry, and give up on school, meaningful work, and themselves, and can fail to realize their potential.

Signs of Giftedness

How do you tell if your child is gifted? Some schools or a private therapist can help you find out for sure, but in general, gifted children:

- Are inquisitive, asking lots of questions, including ethical ones.
- Are usually opinionated, having strong feelings.
- May not be pleased with themselves or their work because they are perfectionists or critical of themselves.
- Often become bored in school and with schoolwork if they know the answers before the "busy work" part is complete.
- Often grasp concepts before skills, so they might skip crucial steps in their education.
- Focus more on understanding the concepts than memorizing the facts. They think abstractly.
- Are creative. These children have active imaginations and solve problems in new ways and/or display artistic talent.
- Can focus for long periods of time on something that they are interested in.
- Are often emotionally sensitive.
- Enjoy puzzles, analogies, and word problems.
- Have a sense of humor that is more complex or developed than other children their age.
- May prefer the company of older children or adults to the company of children their own age.

Coding, Handwriting, and Left-Handedness

Gifted children often have trouble with orthographic (spelling) and phonological (sound representation) "coding." In lay terms, this means that some children have difficulties figuring out spelling rules and patterns, or they may have difficulties figuring out which letters stand for which sounds and when. This can be particularly problematic in English, which requires learning dozens, if not hundreds of spelling rules and exceptions to those rules. Remember the saying "*I* before *E*, except after *C*, or if it sounds like *A* as in 'neighbor' and 'way'"? Such convoluted rules are overwhelming for some kids, and most of the rules don't have convenient, mnemonic rhymes like this one.

 Question

Why is my gifted child's handwriting so sloppy?
Gifted children often focus on the big picture, and details like neatness may seem like a nuisance. But if the child has trouble coding, writing neatly may be extremely difficult and time-consuming. Get to the bottom of the issue before you punish the child for sloppiness or laziness.

Compared to the rest of the population, there is a high number of left-handed people in the "above average" intelligence category. If your gifted child is left-handed or ambidextrous, you should give your child extra consideration when it comes to sloppy handwriting. A child who is gifted may be already frustrated with school, and if the child is also left-handed, he may be struggling to write and do other fine-motor tasks, such as use scissors, within a system that is backward to him. If this is the case, talk to your child and work on brainstorming possible solutions, such as making audio recordings of the answers to homework, or transcribing finished work. Finally, if sloppy handwriting does not get in the way of your child's grades or comprehension, talk to your child about focusing the effort on handwriting on assignments where it counts and letting it slide the rest of the time. *Never try to force a left-handed child to be right-handed.*

Boredom and Anger

The biggest impediment to a gifted child's education, however, is boredom. School is for learning. If your gifted child is not learning in school, something is wrong and should be fixed before the child grows bored and then angry, which can lead to defiant behavior. You should talk to both your child and her teacher if the child is bored and not learning in class. With the teacher, be a sweet pain in the side, and try to find out if she is using differentiated learning, a system in which the same concept is taught in different ways. To your child, you can explain that he doesn't have to like schoolwork, but he still has to do it—that's an important lesson to learn. However, the younger your child is, the more easily this lesson will break down, especially if the teacher is just assigning busy work, so don't rely on that philosophy by itself.

"Gifted kids are at risk for a lot," says Dessery Hensley, who recommends looking into a gifted program or parents' advocacy group. Find out what programs your school and state offer. A good starting point is the National Association for Gifted Children, *www.nagc.org*.

Getting Your Child's Perspective

For some parents, especially those with an authoritarian parenting view, their child's perspective may not seem like an important part of the picture at school—rules should be followed, teachers should be obeyed, and disciplinary action should be upheld. While this is true, the unfortunate truth is that sometimes the child's not at fault, and adults at school are failing to meet his needs academically or otherwise.

Stress Indicators

Your child may not come right out and tell you if something is going wrong at school, either because she's embarrassed, afraid of getting in trouble with you, unsure that what's going on is wrong, or how to articulate it. If you see indicators of stress, such as chewing on the collar of her shirt, biting her nails, sucking on the ends of her hair, or nervous tics like blinking, shoulder shrugging, or frequent swallowing, don't punish her for them, as that will only make matters worse.

 Alert

Tics are not voluntary! Do not punish your child for tics, as any attempt to stop tics increases their frequency. Tics are extremely common and usually disappear on their own within a few years. However, if your child has multiple tics, or the tics interfere with her ability to function, ask your pediatrician for an evaluation.

Find time for some quiet, low-stress bonding, and little by little, ask how school is going and whether your child likes school, the other kids, and the teacher. If your child replies that she doesn't like school, her classmates, or her teacher, don't negate what she says; ask why and take it seriously.

Observing for a Day

Visit your child's school for a day and observe the classroom in action. While it may be difficult to take time off work and you may find it boring and inconvenient, it's a crucial part of finding out more about what's going on at school. Pick a normal school day (not a field trip or the day after Halloween), let the teacher know ahead of time that you'll be coming, and sit in the back of the classroom and don't participate, just observe. You may do this as frequently as you wish; public schools are required to let parents observe. Consider changing schools if your child's school does not allow you to observe; you must know what's going on if you are to help your child.

A Plan for Responding to Defiance

If you've ruled out or resolved any special needs or situations that could influence your child's behavior, you must respond to the defiance or run the risk of sending your child a message that he's not responsible for his behavior. Here are a few tips for responding to defiant behavior at school.

Daily Reports

Ask your child's teacher if he can institute a daily report system with you in which he gives you a brief daily report of behavior. A simple note with one sentence like "Trouble sitting still today," is sufficient and will tell you a lot and help you compare behavior from day to day. Your child can participate in this by adding a sentence of his own; a very young child can draw a happy face or sad face.

Upholding Rules and Consequences

As stated before, you'll need to uphold the school's rules and consequences. If your child's defiant behavior has gotten him in trouble and you have ruled out or resolved special needs, don't try to dig him out of the school's detention policy or defend his behavior to the teacher; uphold the consequences.

Suspension and Expulsion

You'll need to uphold rules and consequences even if they are severe. If your child is suspended or expelled, education *must* continue. Find out the standards for your child's grade, and keep the child up to speed on schoolwork at home or with a tutor. The school may have suggestions on how to keep your child educated in the interim, so be sure to ask. Finally, school should not be replaced with screen time. If your child is at home because of disciplinary action, letting him watch TV or play on the computer all day could seem like a reward, so require him to keep up with schoolwork and make a list of chores to do if you must be at work.

Being on Your Child's Side

One of the most important lessons you can teach your child as a parent is that you are on her team, and that you're on her side for life, no matter what she does. This doesn't mean you always agree with her, it means you'll do what's in her best interests because you're the parent and care about her development. Here's how to do that with respect to trouble at school.

Making the Most of School Resources

If you don't ask, you'll never know. Ask questions to find out what services the school, district, and state offer. Just because you haven't heard about them, or because no one's using them, doesn't mean they don't exist. "Is tutoring available?" "Can my child use the computers in the library after school?" "Is there a job skills training program?" "How do we sign up for a college fair?" "Is there a gang prevention program?" and so on may uncover resources you didn't know existed. Jump online and find out if the state or district offer services at your child's school, or make an appointment with a counselor at the district level. If there's little help available, try your city or county offices, which may offer more.

When to Change Teachers

Up until sixth grade, a teacher who is punitive, insults you or your child, pressures the child too hard, or refuses to meet your child's educational needs is not creating a healthy learning environment for your child. If the teacher's behavior is severe or has not changed after a few interventions on your part, change classes. However, once the child reaches about sixth grade, you need to teach her to get along with all kinds of people, even those who don't like her, so an older child should remain in the class unless the situation is severe.

When to Organize with Other Parents

Much of school policy exists because parents and voters asked for it. With this in mind, if you don't like something at your child's school, find out if there is an existing parents' advocacy group for dealing with the problem. Advocacy groups exist for all kinds of situations, from the general PTA/PTO organizations to distinct associations for children with special needs. If there's not already an organization that fills your need, find out if there are other parents who are sharing your experience, and start an organization of your own. For example, some parent groups have recently succeeded in making schools set homework time limits to keep elementary school children from having excessive homework. Remember that parents have a lot of power.

Alternative Education Options

Sometimes, a child can't go to school, either because it has ceased to be an environment for learning, because she is being sent to continuation, or because a teen girl has had a baby and can't be at school all day. If your child cannot or should not go to school anymore—and if you have used the tips in this chapter to try to make the best learning environment possible—don't let that be the end of your child's education. Don't rule out higher education in the future, either. Find out if your district offers independent study, job skills training programs, adult ed courses, or a system through which your child can take a high school equivalency exam and earn units to get into a college or university.

CHAPTER 18

Traumatic Experiences

A final factor to consider when dealing with a defiant child is whether your child has been exposed to a traumatic experience. It's terrible to think that your child, whom you love very much, may have been exposed to trauma at some point, but it's important not to ignore this topic if you are to help your child grow and develop healthily, because trauma can have lasting impacts on a child's cognitive and emotional functioning. If you are the parent of a child who has been abused, or who has been adopted or in foster care, or who has lived in other homes besides your own, it is especially important to consider this issue.

How Trauma Affects Children

Dr. Bruce Perry is a leading authority on children and trauma. During a lecture, he once asked listeners whether children are "sponges"—absorbing everything from their environments—or if they are resilient, with bad experiences harmlessly bouncing off of them. They can't be both, he reasoned. The answer? Children are more like sponges. "Children are resilient" is more apt when it comes to healing *physically*, as from a broken leg or the flu. In reality, life experiences make profound psychological effects on children.

Brain Functioning

When children are exposed to violence or are threatened in any way, they may regress, that is, act less than their age. An example common to most parents' experience is a relapse in potty training skills after the child experiences a stressful event. Other common examples are thumb sucking, or reliance on a "blankie" or other security object, or clinging to the parent.

However, it goes deeper than just these obvious visible signs, because regression is a symptom of less complex brain activity, of cognitive functioning happening in the brain stem, rather than the cerebral cortex. (Note that higher-order mammals have a cerebral cortex and a brain stem, while reptiles and lower-order animals have mostly a stem.) When a child or adult feels threatened or fearful, the animal instincts for protection kick in from the brain stem, and reason can go out the window as the person focuses on surviving.

 Essential

The brain's need to direct activity parallels the discussion of Maslow's Hierarchy of Needs in Chapter 2. Just as a person can't be focused on staying alive and on self-actualization at the same time, a brain can't be thinking complex, abstract thoughts while the animal response to danger is kicking in. That's why writing an essay is difficult for a child living in fear.

This instinct works extremely well at helping people and animals survive, but it comes at a price: the more it happens, and the more a child lives in an aroused or fearful state of mind, the more brain pathways are strengthened for reacting to threat in an instinctual, rather than reasonable way. In fact, after this goes on for a while, what seems like minor provocation to someone else can be read by the child as a threat, and the child can react with violence.

Emotional Functioning: Attachment Revisited

In Chapter 2, you also learned about attachment, which is more than just a nice feeling but a theory that states that children need a strong relationship with a primary adult caregiver in order for normal development to take place. If the child is bounced from one caregiver to another, or has a caregiver who abuses or neglects him, or who simply fails to respond to his physical or emotional needs, a disorder known as Reactive Attachment Disorder (RAD), or an insecure or disorganized attachment style can develop. A child with these problems may fail to engage in social interactions, or conversely may over-engage by acting as if everybody is his friend and trusting strangers. Of course, the child will still strive to meet basic needs from the bottom of the hierarchy, including for teens the need for sexual intimacy, and this can lead to inappropriate sexual relationships.

Understanding Post-Traumatic Stress Disorder

Post-Traumatic Stress Disorder (PTSD) is an anxiety disorder that results from an event in which severe physical harm occurred, or was threatened, or where the person witnessed physical harm or a severe threat to a loved one. In military veterans, PTSD is also called "combat stress." PTSD can be found in refugees from war-torn areas, rape victims, people who have lived through natural disasters or terrible accidents, victims of violent crime, and children who have been abused or witnessed abuse. It can also result from severe psychological/emotional trauma.

Symptoms and Diagnosis

PTSD is characterized by the following symptoms, which are used as criteria for diagnosis:

- Exposure to a traumatic event
- Intrusive memories of the event (flashbacks)

- Avoidance (the child avoids triggers or stimuli associated with the traumatic event)
- Decreased general responsiveness (the child feels detached, sees a bleak future or early death, is uninterested in participating in significant activities)
- Hyper-arousal (is hyper-vigilant, startles easily, has trouble falling asleep, difficulty concentrating)
- The symptoms above interfere with normal functioning.

As you can see, these symptoms make abstract thought difficult. It's very hard for a child exposed to trauma to concentrate and do well on schoolwork, so she shouldn't be punished for bad grades. These symptoms also must persist for more than a month in order to meet the criteria for diagnosis. Note that it is common for the symptoms to begin several months after the traumatic event.

Treatment

The most effective proven treatment for PTSD is therapy, specifically cognitive therapy. Group therapy is also effective; teens may benefit greatly from sharing with other teens who have had similar experiences, though this may not be feasible with young children. Medication has also been shown to have an effect, though it is rare for medication to cure PTSD on its own. Make sure any medication prescribed for a child has been approved for children. As with any treatment program, ask to see a track record for the recommended treatment course, and verify that the people running the program are licensed professionals following a proven plan.

Types of Abuse

Child abuse is, undoubtedly, a traumatic experience. In order to be child abuse, the act must be perpetrated by a person who is charged with the child's care, such as a parent or babysitter. There are several types of abuse: neglect and verbal, psychological/emotional, physical, and sexual abuse. Witnessing domestic violence can also be construed as child abuse. Read on—you might be surprised to find out which type of abuse is the most common.

Neglect—The Most Common Form of Child Abuse

According to *Speaking Up: How to Help the Children You Work with Who Live in Abusive Homes*, the most common form of child abuse is neglect: an astounding 60 percent of child abuse cases involve neglect. This is a number that has been relatively constant over the years.

 Fact

Recent data from the federal government show that a combination of maltreatment types, such as neglect and physical abuse together, is the most common factor in child abuse fatalities. However, neglect is the most common single factor in child abuse fatalities; about 34 percent of the fatalities were attributable to neglect alone.

Neglect is a "sin of omission." It's the failure of a parent or caregiver to act. This can range from a lack of supervision—leaving a small child in the bathtub or a six-year-old to care for himself overnight—to not providing adequate nourishment, clothing, or medical care despite the ability to do so.

Other Types of Abuse

Other types of abuse include:

- Verbal abuse: yelling, name-calling, insults, telling a child to shut up.
- Psychological/emotional abuse: threats, harsh and constant criticism, rejection, abandonment, withholding love, support,

or guidance. Since all other forms of abuse have a traumatic psychological/emotional effect, they can also fit under this category.

- Physical abuse: Hitting, pushing, throwing objects at a child, burning a child, choking, shaking, whipping.
- Sexual abuse: incest, rape, fondling a child's genitals, penetration, sodomy, indecent exposure, exploitation (includes child prostitution or production of pornographic materials featuring children).

Warning Signs of Abuse

If you share child care with another caregiver, such as an ex-spouse or babysitter, or if you are taking over care of a child who previously lived with other caregivers—if you recently began caring for a stepchild or foster child, or have adopted—then it's possible your child has been abused by another caregiver. Child advocates are sometimes accused of arousing unwarranted suspicion; while it's true that sensational media reports stir people into a frenzy, child abuse is a serious and all-too-frequent problem that deserves attention, prevention, and intervention. Nearly one million children are the victims of abuse or neglect each year in the United States. If you are concerned your child may have been or is being abused, take a look at these warning signs of abuse to see if there is a pattern emerging.

Warning Signs of Neglect

Except for blatant signs of physical abuse such as a bruised neck that indicates strangulation, warning signs of abuse are usually subtle and can indicate other problems and stressors that you've read about earlier in this book. For that reason, in the absence of a serious physical injury or immediate danger, it's important to look for *a pattern of behaviors* before taking action as described in the next section. The warnings signs of abuse are adapted from *Speak-*

ing Up: How to Help the Children You Work with Who Live in Abusive Homes.

- Unkempt, poor hygiene
- Inappropriate dress for the weather (shorts in winter, overcoat in summer)
- Unmet medical or dental needs, especially when the family has the means to provide adequate medical care
- Routinely hungry and thirsty (more so than is to be expected from daily activities) or reports not having had meals
- Fatigue and lethargy
- Lack of basic emotional and intellectual skills
- Unusually thin, weak, or of poor muscle development
- Chapped lips and skin on a regular basis
- Reports being left alone for long periods of time

Young Children (Ages 0-5)

Young children may have trouble articulating what's bothering them, or may have been told they can't disclose something because it's a secret. Please take all disclosures of abuse seriously and take action as described later in this chapter. Note that many of these behaviors can be classified as "regressive."

- Bruises, cuts, burns, or unexplained injuries
- Trouble sitting or moving
- Acts out violently and inappropriately
- Easily frustrated
- Refusal to cooperate with instructions or participate in group activities
- Withdrawal from social life
- Difficulty learning and paying attention
- Delayed verbal development
- Poor motor skills, lack of coordination

- Psychosomatic symptoms (frequent headaches and stomachaches) and lack of bowel/bladder control, especially in new environments or around new people
- Difficulty sleeping
- Insecurity, clinginess
- Anxiety
- Disclosure of abuse. *Please take all disclosures of abuse seriously.*

Older Children

Again, look for a *pattern of behavior* rather than a one-time instance since these symptoms can indicate other problems as well, as discussed in the section titled "The Markers" in Chapter 12.

- Difficulty learning and paying attention; poor grades
- Low self-esteem
- Aggressive behavior
- The homicidal triad
- Other violent outbursts
- Bullying
- Social withdrawal
- Poor social skills
- Clinginess
- Psychosomatic symptoms (frequent headaches and stomachaches)
- Anxiety
- Property destruction and vandalism
- Reckless, risk-taking behavior
- Inability to express feelings
- Drug/alcohol use
- Bullying
- Involvement in abusive dating relationships

Warning Signs of Teen Dating Violence

Teen dating violence (including physical and nonphysical types of abuse) is extremely common in our society. Children who are abused or controlled at home often go on to mimic these behaviors in their own abusive romantic relationships. Here are the warning signs for teen dating violence; some apply more to the abuser than the victim, and vice versa.

- Presence of a dating relationship (may be heterosexual or homosexual)
- Low self-esteem
- Anxiety
- Violent outbursts
- Property destruction
- Reckless behavior
- Lying to parents and authorities, sneaking around with boy/girlfriend
- Controlling behaviors
- Trying to be perfect
- Cutting class
- Psychosomatic symptoms
- Clinginess
- Inability to express feelings
- Alcohol/drug use
- Victim is socially isolated from friends or previously enjoyable activities

Most teens will *not* want to leave an abusive dating relationship. Dr. Jill Murray is the nation's leading expert on teen dating violence; see her book *But I Love Him* for more information.

What to Do about Ongoing Abuse

It is terrifying to suspect or realize that your child is being abused. If you think your child is currently being abused by another caretaker, there are some specific actions you can take to intervene and keep your child safe, and there are also things you should *not* do.

Dos

Understand that the child will be very fearful of retaliation, and that you must treat this subject delicately. Talk to your child using the tips below about what's going on. If a child discloses abuse, tell him he has done the right thing by telling you about it, and that you love him very much. Gather as much information as you can without alerting the person you suspect of abusing the child, who may retaliate against the child if found out. If you suspect abuse by a hired caregiver, take your child out of the situation by finding a new caregiver immediately, and make a child abuse report with Child Protective Services (CPS) or local law enforcement to minimize the danger to other children in the person's care.

 Question

How do I make a child abuse report?
You may make a child abuse report by calling local law enforcement or your local CPS agency; numbers for each can be found on the Internet and these agencies share reports with each other. You can also call Childhelp's National Child Abuse Hotline at 1-800-4-A-CHILD.

If you suspect abuse by a family member from whose care you can remove the child—say, an older cousin entrusted to babysit—remove the child from that person's care immediately and consider getting a restraining order and filing a child abuse report, especially if the person is still caring for other children. However, if the person is someone you share custody with—an estranged spouse, ex-spouse, or stepparent, for example—restraining orders and child abuse reports are necessary, but you may need to enlist the help of an attorney to make sure you take all necessary steps to help your child. Most counties and states have a bar association where you can find free or low-cost legal help.

Finally, whenever you feel the child is in immediate or serious danger, *call 911 immediately.*

Don'ts

Don't do any detective work on your own: you might alert the perpetrator, which can result in further abuse, you might engage in criminal activity that could jeopardize your status as a competent caretaker for the child, or you might interfere with a law enforcement investigation. So don't follow anyone, stalk anyone, or try to take pictures or video of a suspected abuser.

Do not keep abuse a secret. Don't ignore a child who discloses abuse. Don't worry that the child will be removed from your care (this is extremely rare and is not CPS's desired course of action). Don't worry that the child will hate you for taking action—it's better to have a child feel safe and secure in your care, forming a strong attachment, than a child who feels temporarily that you're cool, which does not form a strong attachment.

How to Talk to Your Child

To initiate a conversation, find a quiet time when the two of you are alone, tell the child you love him, state what you've noticed, and ask for input: "I love you very much and I'm worried about something. I've noticed that after you come home from so-and-so's house, you're often quiet and have a stomachache. Is something happening there that bothers you?" Allow your child plenty of time—from thirty seconds to a whole week—to answer the question. Say, "If there's anything happening that you don't like or that you think is wrong, no matter what it is, you can tell me about it anytime, and I'll listen." Revisit the conversation if need be. If your child doesn't disclose anything, but you are still suspicious of a hired caretaker, come home early or show up at the daycare facility and observe. If you are suspicious of a family member with whom you have custody, you can ask an attorney what your options are.

During and after a disclosure use empathetic listening skills explained in Chapter 8. Affirm your love for your child by saying so: "I love you." Tell the child you are always glad to see him, and assure him that he has done the right thing by telling you, and that you will do everything you can to help him. Tell him that the abuse is wrong, and that it is not his fault in any way. Tell a younger child that you will talk to some other grown-ups about how to solve the problem, and that you will let him know how it's going (by advising him about changes in caretakers ahead of time and doing all you can to make the transition easy as described in Chapter 2) and do whatever it takes to keep him safe. Tell an older child that in order for the abuse to stop, you must do something about it, and offer him the chance to participate in reporting and talking to an attorney or law enforcement by either talking to the officials or by being present and holding your hand while you do the talking.

Violence in Your Own Home

If you are experiencing domestic violence in your own home, be aware that exposure to the trauma of domestic violence can legally be construed as psychological child abuse. Kids can hear what's going on and are definitely affected by watching parents yell at or hit each other, and kids begin to suffer the cognitive and emotional consequences described at the beginning of this chapter. If you are in an abusive marriage as the perpetrator or victim, please get help immediately for the sake of your children as well as yourself and your spouse.

If you are concerned that you or your partner might hurt your children, you are in need of extra support. Your county human services or social services can help you, and so can law enforcement, so call 911 in an emergency and do an Internet search for your county's social services in a nonemergency. Many services are free.

How to Help a Traumatized Child Feel Secure and Loved

A child who has been traumatized by abuse, abandonment, or witnessing a violent crime or scary situation needs to feel safe. As the caregiver, the best way to express your love and good intent for the child is to create a safe, secure, and consistent environment, in both a physical and emotional sense.

Physically Safe

Helping a child feel physically safe is easier than making the child feel emotionally safe. Be lenient about security blankets and allow a child to stay physically close to you, especially at bedtime. Remember what it was like when you were a child and the house seemed so much bigger—if your child's room is far away from yours, can you set the child up in your own bedroom for awhile? Let the child know you are just a few feet away at all times and permit clinginess; don't punish regression. If you think the child won't exhibit violent tendencies, a dog can provide an added level of security and physical comfort for the child; research a breed that is gentle and loyal and fits your family's lifestyle.

 Fact

Physical proximity and visibility are very important to people who have been abused; some domestic violence shelters and charitable foundations design homes for abused parents in which the living space is so open that they can see their children at all times. An example can be found at *www.nicoleshouse.org*.

In addition, try to minimize disturbing noises, such as violent television programs or fast-paced music, when the child is home, whether she's awake or asleep. If you live in a noisy neighborhood, getting a white noise fan or a small fountain for the child's bedroom can help establish a peaceful vibe.

Emotionally Safe

It's more difficult to help a child feel emotionally safe, but you can do it by following these tips. *The most important thing to do is respect and accept the child's feelings.* Have conversations about feelings and the child's experiences when she wants to, not when you want to. Normalize the feelings: however the child feels is perfectly valid; don't negate feelings of hate or anger. Tell the child you love her and remind her often that being abused or traumatized is not her fault, and that she is not responsible for any tragic or traumatic events that have occurred. Encourage her to express her feelings through talking, drawing, artwork. Help the child process the feelings by asking "what if" questions such as, "So what if you could . . . ? What would you do then?"

Continue working on feelings until you get to the core of the child's feelings, and you will often find that the child feels hurt or wronged in some way, and address this feeling. You can address the feeling through prayer, by writing a letter that never gets mailed, and so on. In addition, the child may greatly benefit from therapy, which can often be had for a low cost at a domestic violence shelter.

Disciplining an Abused Child

An abused child may understandably have a lot of anger and sorrow to work through, and as such may try to test the boundaries a little more than other children. Set rules and boundaries, and be prepared to make an art form out of knowing when it's necessary to be consistent and when you can be flexible. An important part of consistency is to refrain from changing rules on the spur of the moment—only change them after you've talked about it and written it up on your rule chart. Finally, do not harshly criticize an abused child or discipline her in a way that resembles how she was abused, which means you must *never* grab, hit, or slap the hand of an abused child (the only exception is grabbing the child to save her from immediate physical danger).

Special Considerations for Adopted and Foster Children

Adopted and foster children are at increased risk for RAD and have difficulty bonding because, with the exception of an infant adopted at birth, their bonds have been severed. As the new caregiver, you must consider your own perception of the child in addition to the child's perception of you and his world.

Adoption, Foster Care, and Trauma

If you want the child to have an emotionally healthy life, you must be a reliable and emotionally available caregiver for the child. Consider what it would be like for the child if he thought that you could get rid of him at any moment, just as easily as you took him in. Being available for the long haul and making the child's emotional needs a priority is the best way to provide a reliable and emotionally available caregiving environment. However, it's not easy, and once the child knows he is safe, he will probably need to work through his feelings of anger and abandonment, meaning you will have a cycle (or many) of feelings and behaviors to work through.

How to Bond as the New Caregiver

Be emotionally available consistently, and don't go back on your word. If you say, "Let's go to the park tomorrow!" stick to it, because this child has been let down before. Make life as predictable as possible, and pay close emotional attention to him. What kinds of events or emotions are pleasant for the child? What seems to disturb him? Minimize the bad; maximize the good, and talk when the child wants to, not when you want to.

Healing from Abuse and Trauma

To heal from abuse and trauma takes a lot of love, time, and attention. Therapy can be quite helpful. If you find that it makes the child feel like the identified patient, or like there is something wrong with her, try family therapy instead. It can help the child feel like you're on her team, an important way to give her a little extra support.

Positive Reinforcement

Be very kind, loving, and gentle with a child who has been abused or traumatized, and follow the tips for praise and reward outlined in Chapter 5. Continue catching the child in the act of doing something good and respond with "Way to go!" a hug, or a reward.

Time

Healing from abuse and trauma takes a lot of time, and depending on the severity of the experience, may never be complete. You *can* affect the child for the better, though. Be patient and consistent, and show a lot of love. It's not possible to spoil a child with love! Love doesn't mean giving her everything she wants, it means being affectionate in a way that the child appreciates, and providing a safe and emotionally stable environment.

CHAPTER 19

Help and Support for Yourself

Everything you've been dealing with to help your defiant child has no doubt been stressful for you. Your feelings have probably ranged all over the emotional spectrum, from frustration to anger to sadness to worry. Such feelings take a toll. In order to parent effectively, you need to have some "juice" left in your batteries, and that means getting help and support for yourself. Taking time to recharge doesn't mean you are ditching your responsibilities and taking a break doesn't mean you're off gallivanting irresponsibly; self-care is essential to living healthy and being strong for your kids.

Your Self-Image: The Authority Role Revisited

Back in Chapter 1, you learned about different parenting styles: permissive, dictatorial, and authoritative. Hopefully, this book has given you an array of tools and skills that you can employ in an authoritative parenting style—one that is neither permissive (letting your kid do whatever he pleases) nor dictatorial (controlling everything, with no questions asked). That doesn't mean you'll be totally comfortable using them—yet.

Confidence

Once you have decided on a course of action, whether it's how to set up a star chart, which therapist to choose for your child, or when to get a restraining order, you must be confident in your decision. Trust that you are acting in your child's best interests to the best of your ability and move forward. There's a difference between changing your mind because new information has come forward (rescinding discipline for bad grades when you find out your child has a learning disability) and changing your mind because you're unsure of yourself (waffling when your child whines about consequences). It's okay to question whether you're doing the right thing—everybody does, and nobody knows—and it's wise to realize there's always something new to learn, but a certain amount of confidence is essential to staying sane and setting a good example.

The Perfect Parent

Part of staying sane is also realizing that you can't be perfect, and you can't raise a perfect child, because quite simply, perfection does not exist. The goal shouldn't be to raise a child who conforms to or exceeds the status quo, or even is the "best" he can be; it should be to raise a child who becomes a healthy, satisfied adult with the necessary skills to manage the many obstacles and trials life will throw his way.

How to Deal with Others' Judgment of Your Child

Since nobody can be perfect, at some point your children will misbehave in public, at school, or in front of someone you'd like to impress, or whose criticism you fear. In the midst of a behavior problem, a tongue-clucking stranger who says, "Kids these days! You never used to hear back talk like that!" can frustrate and annoy a parent who's doing her best, and perhaps even bring her to tears. Here's how to deal with what other people think.

Turn the Lens Around

Oftentimes, a person's criticism says more about himself than it does about the critiqued: when a stranger complains about "noisy brats," there's more to the comment than the insult you're likely to hear first. There's also information in that comment about his own tendency to judge people and call names. If you think about it, the person could also be cluing you in to feelings, which could be any of the following: "I can't hear over the kids' yelling," "I feel like my personal space is invaded," or "I miss being around kids I know and love." Noticing underlying messages will show you how futile it would be to get into a shouting match over whether or not your kids are noisy brats. It's a no-win situation.

 Alert

If you want—and this will depend on the situation and the person— you can use effective communication skills to turn this kind of interaction into a positive one. You can say something like, "It sounds like the noise is disturbing you," and see if further comments point in the direction of a solution.

Remember that you don't have to take such a message to heart; in fact, such insults are a sure-fire way to hurt a parent's feelings. Don't internalize insults, and remember the saying "The people who matter don't mind, and the people who mind don't matter." While others' feelings *are* valid, you don't have to engage in a dialogue with someone who is insulting you, especially when the person is a total stranger.

Cold Consideration

Now and then, a caring loved one or tactful stranger might venture forth with real, constructive criticism. Sometimes, the person will take you aside and say, "I wanted to talk to you about something. . . ." Other times, the person may be so fearful of upsetting you that she'll just drop a subtle comment into the conversation, such as "Do you think Zach might need to get his hearing checked?" When another person is doing her best to be respectful and courteous, try to listen openly and thank the person, even though it's hard. Later, you can decide whether the comment is valid, and you might even wish to bounce the comment off others you trust. Still, keep a "cold" eye on the problem, try not to become angry or saddened until you get to the bottom of the situation.

How to Select Your Support Network

Chapter 8 gave some starting points for how to deal with extended family issues. Many people believe it takes a village to raise a child. Here's how to assemble your "village" into three tiers for the twenty-first century. Each tier needs careful selection and some nurturing whenever you can manage it.

The First Tier

The first tier of your support network is made up of close family members. If you co-parent with another person, your first tier is pretty obviously made up of you, your co-parent, and your child or children.

If you don't have a partner, you need another dependable *adult*—a close friend, parent, or sibling with whom you don't mind sharing personal information about yourself and your children, and who can be physically available, at least sometimes, to help with caring for the child. It may help to say this in so many words: "I'm really grateful for all you've been doing to help me, because I'd never be able to raise my family on my own. You are the one person I know I can count on more than anybody else. How does that feel to you?"

The Second Tier

The second tier of your support network can include extended family members, trusted friends and neighbors, and family who lives farther away. These are people who care about the child, even love the child, and provide support in a sporadic or limited way.

You don't have to share everything with the second tier—perhaps these people don't need to know about sensitive medical or personal issues—but you do need to keep them informed about what's going on with the child, *and also keep the child connected to them* via visits and phone calls.

The Third Tier

The third tier is less emotionally connected to the child and your parenting. These are people who provide professional services—teachers, principals, therapists, doctors, and government agencies—or people who lend a hand indirectly or who might help in an emergency (a fitness instructor, a parent of your child's friend, a coworker you're just getting to know, a neighbor you keep in contact with sporadically).

What to Share with Your Child about Your Own Life

If you have suffered some particularly tough challenges in life (which is probably most people), then you need to share these with your child and with other people. It's a matter of choosing the right people to talk to at the right times. If your need to talk is more for self-healing, please be aware of this and seek out therapy, as it will help you to unload on an adult and then make better decisions about what to share with your child and when.

Appropriate Stories, Appropriate Moments

For the most part, share funny, happy, and silly stories from your own childhood with your child. Think about what you enjoyed, what your favorite games were, your favorite foods, your favorite books, your favorite songs, your favorite places, an interesting picture your family had on the wall that you might be able to dig up on the Internet and print out for your child. These are the things to share freely. Share them at an age-appropriate time—stories about your positive experiences in grade school are most suitable for sharing with your grade-schooler.

 Alert

Be careful about holding up an impossible ideal, or using stories that compare yourself to your child, with you coming out on top. If your high schooler just missed an important shot in a basketball game, don't share your own story of how you won the state championship with a last-second three-pointer. Kids are very sensitive to shaming and to feeling inferior.

If You Were Abused or Suffered

It is okay to tell your children about what you've been through if you have already gotten professional help, there is a constructive reason for sharing, and you scaffold the experiences at age-appropriate times so you only share information your child can handle. For example, if you were sexually abused, you can use your experience to make sure you talk to your young child about appropriate touching. Later, you can use this to inform your child about how to recognize when she's not comfortable around somebody. Much later, when your child is a teen, you can explain that the reason you have never left her alone with a certain family member is because that person abused you, and that's the reason you don't want your child going to that person's house alone.

If You Are in an Abusive Relationship Now

Domestic violence is all too common in our society. Not only does it affect your own quality of life, it affects your child's quality of life now and in the future. It is all right if you feel love toward an abusive partner, and you may be able to stay in the relationship long-term, but *you must not ignore the problem*, because abuse will not get better without professional help.

Identifying an Abusive Relationship

Your relationship is abusive if the following behavior patterns are occurring:

- Your partner yells at you, calls you names, insults you, lies to you, makes fun of you, or tells you to shut up.
- Your partner plays mind games with you, makes you feel bad about yourself, controls your money, destroys your belongings, impedes your education, career, or other goals, hurts your pet, or threatens to do any of the above.
- You feel like your partner controls your life.
- Your partner hits, pushes, scratches, or burns you, or throws things at you.
- Your partner rapes you or forces you to engage in sexual activities you're not comfortable with.
- Your partner has isolated you from your family and friends, discourages you from being active and involved, or has kept you from participating in social activities.
- Your relationship goes through a cycle of explosive incidents, making up, and building tension.
- You feel like you're walking on eggshells around your partner, and that the littlest thing could set your partner off.
- Your partner threatens to commit suicide if you ever leave.

- Your partner stalks you or threatens to hurt or kill you, your children, or others you care about.

If You Are an Abuser

If, in reading the warning signs above, you recognize your own behaviors, seek help from a licensed therapist. Admitting that you have a problem is very admirable because it takes a lot of courage, and it is the first step toward fixing the situation. Chances are, you have been through a great deal of pain in your own life. By taking action to help yourself, you can spare your own partner and children the same experiences. Confronting your feelings can be scary. Courage is the path to being a *true* hero for your family. You are not destined to repeat the past.

Your Options

If you are being abused, you have several options, depending on how serious your situation is. If you fear for your or your children's lives, it's time to call 911 immediately. If you are being abused but you and your children are not in immediate danger, reach out to a trusted friend or loved one who you know will *not* tell your partner you've talked about the situation. *Abuse usually escalates if the abuser finds out the victim has talked about what is going on. Do not let the abuser know you have reached out.* You can call your county's social services department from your loved one's house and ask what your options are. If you have time, you can gather important papers before going to a shelter. Most counties have one, if not several, domestic violence shelters where you and your children can stay while you get counseling, find a job, and get on your feet. Many counties also have services for boarding pets so that you don't have to leave your pet in the abuser's care.

Impact on Your Child

As you read earlier, children can hear domestic violence, even when they're in their rooms and supposed to be sleeping, and witnessing abuse has a traumatic effect on them, which, as you now know, can affect their cognitive and emotional development. It's crucial to your child's development to get help. Holding a family together makes sense if it's in the child's best interests; it doesn't if it is harmful to the child. In addition, people grow accustomed to their environments; if your child grows up in an abusive home, she is highly likely to seek out an abusive romantic relationship later in life.

How to Move Forward from Past Pain

By this point, you have learned many skills for how to parent a defiant child. Now, it is time to move forward from past pain, whether it's a painful divorce, a traumatic experience, or just the stress of parenting a defiant child. There are ways to do this that are good for you and your family, and ways that are harmful.

The Dangers of Self-Medicating

"Self-medicating" means taking it upon yourself to ingest substances to make you feel better. This might be using old prescriptions, someone else's prescriptions, or lying to a doctor about your symptoms to get a medication you want. Or, it could mean using drugs or alcohol to escape from painful situations and memories. Self-medicating is very dangerous. Do not take any medication that has not been specifically prescribed for you by a physician for real and relevant symptoms. Self-medicating with alcohol, drugs, food, dangerous sex, or any other substance or activity used in excess to numb pain is very dangerous.

People also self-medicate using other dangerous and addictive behaviors, such as gambling, unsafe sex, overeating, and so on. If you want to stop an addiction, get professional support and replace the addiction with a healthy activity you can sustain long-term, as many people transfer from one addiction to another; for example, after bariatric surgery, many patients become addicted to alcohol or gambling instead of food.

 Fact

> Endorphins are your brain's homemade pain relievers. These compounds are produced in the brain and create feelings of well-being similar to opiate drugs. Endorphins are produced during all sorts of activities, from sex and strenuous exercise to excitement and danger. Stick to healthy activities to get your "natural high," such as exercise or safe sex with a trusted partner.

How to Self-Counsel When You Can't Afford Therapy

Counseling is extremely effective, and highly recommended for parents contending with a number of difficult issues. However, it's not realistic to assume that everyone can afford therapy, or that everyone can afford therapy for multiple family members, or for any one family member long-term. Instead, check out the wealth of amazing self-help books available—you are bound to find several that address any single problem. Support groups are also helpful (remember that they should be facilitated by a licensed professional and follow a program with a proven track record). Finally, the Internet is a great source of information and community, with emotional well-being sites like *www.FeelBetterNetwork.com* providing expert-led services and support groups.

Forming Healthy Coping Behaviors

Everybody needs an outlet. Exercise is a smart way to get some "me time" and produce some endorphins simultaneously. Artistic expression is another way to let off steam. Connecting with friends, getting in touch with nature, reading, meditating, prayer, taking a bath, or simply doing nothing for a few minutes a day are all healthy ways to cope with parenting a defiant child. When you need to recharge, avoid information overload (TV, web surfing), service activities (volunteering at the school), or activities that drain you or feed an obsession (painting the house, political blogging). Note that these activities aren't *bad*, they just aren't effective ways to cope.

Find a healthy way to cope. Take care of yourself. You must recharge so you and your child can live a happier, healthier life.

APPENDIX A

The Markers

In general, the following symptoms are indicative of a range of serious underlying problems in your child—from depression to dating violence to drug use and more—that you should try understand when they persist over a few weeks or more, or when they steadily get worse:

- Abrupt changes in sleeping patterns and appetite (not attributable to a growth spurt)
- Abrupt changes in behavior, or changes in personality
- Abrupt changes in friends
- Reluctance to engage in activities previously enjoyed
- Difficulty concentrating
- Marked decline in school performance
- Irritability
- Unexplained aches and pains
- Unexplained injuries
- Self-inflicted injuries, such as cutting
- Reckless behaviors
- Tearfulness and frequent crying
- Lack of motivation
- Reluctance to go to school
- Restlessness, agitation
- Mood swings (not attributable to hormones)

- Withdrawal
- Strange giddiness or hyperactivity
- Crime
- The homicidal triad (see Chapter 11)
- Reference to or fixation on troublesome behaviors, such as suicide or drug use

Additional Resources

Books

Barkley, Russell and Christine Benton. *Your Defiant Child: Eight Steps to Better Behavior.* (New York, NY: The Guilford Press, 1998).

Diamond, Marian and Janet Hopson. *The Magic Trees of the Mind: How to Nurture Your Child's Intelligence, Creativity, and Healthy Emotions from Birth through Adolescence.* (New York, NY: Plume, 1998).

Garbarina, James and Ellen deLara. *And Words* Can *Hurt Forever: How to Protect Adolescents from Bullying, Harassment, and Emotional Violence.* (New York, NY: The Free Press, 2002).

Hilling, Hogan and Jesse Rutherford. *The Modern Mom's Guide to Dads: Ten Secrets Your Husband Won't Tell You.* (Nashville, TN: Cumberland House Publishing, 2007).

Levin, Diane and Jean Kilbourne. *So Sexy, So Soon: The New Sexualized Childhood and What Parents Can Do to Protect Their Kids.* (New York, NY: Ballantine Books, 2009).

Pinker, Steven. *The Language Instinct: How the Mind Creates Language (P.S.).* (New York, NY: Harper Perennial, 2007).

Postman, Neil and Andrew Postman. *Amusing Ourselves to Death: Public Discourse in the Age of Show Business.* (New York, NY: Penguin, 2005).

Rosenberg, Marshall. *Nonviolent Communication: A Language of Compassion,* 2nd ed. (Encinitas, CA: PuddleDancer Press, 2003).

Rutherford, Jesse, Kathleen Nickerson, and Johanna Kim. *Speaking Up: How to Help the Children You Work with Who Live in Abusive Homes.* (Lincoln, NE: iUniverse, 2006).

Websites

ChildTrauma Academy, a nonprofit organization working to improve the lives of high-risk children through direct service, research, and education. *www.childtrauma.org*

The Feel Better Network, a site with information, support, and answers so people don't have to face emotional challenges alone. *www.feelbetternetwork.com*

Substance Abuse and Mental Health Services Administration (SAMHSA), a division of the United States Department of Health and Human Services with information, resources, and direction to real-world services. *www.samhsa.gov*

National Institute of Mental Health (NIH), research-backed information on mental health. *www.nimh.nih.gov*

Sample Responsibilities and Rewards Worksheet

Note to parents: When using a responsibilities and rewards worksheet, remember that the younger the child, the more immediate and tangible the reward should be. For all children, rewards should be measurable and should not be taken away once earned. A worksheet like this one, posted in a conspicuous place, provides transparent accountability for everyone and helps the child see that your decisions are not random or arbitrary. For children of all ages, select no more than two behaviors to work on at once. *Remember, rewards are much more effective than punishment at changing a child's behavior!*

This sample worksheet is for a child in elementary or middle school. With this particular worksheet, you should carry over any leftover checks from one week into the next. See Chapter 5 for more details on how to implement a rewards system effectively.

MAYA'S REWARD CHART

BEHAVIOR	LEFTOVER CHECKS FROM LAST WEEK	MONDAY	TUESDAY	WEDNESDAY
Complete and turn in homework	0	√	√	√
Play peacefully with sibling for several minutes or more. Being loud is okay. Fighting is not.	1		√	√

THURSDAY	FRIDAY	SATURDAY	SUNDAY	REWARD
√				5 checks = 30 minutes extra screen time
	√			3 checks = choose the menu for a meal

Index